The

PARTY BIBLE

The PARTY BIBLE

The Good Book for Great Times

Connor Pritchard and Dominic Russo
founders of The 5th Year and co-creators of *Workaholics*

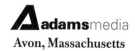

adamsmedia
Avon, Massachusetts

Published by
Adams Media, a division of F+W Media, Inc.
57 Littlefield Street, Avon, MA 02322. U.S.A.
www.adamsmedia.com

ISBN 10: 1-4405-0595-0
ISBN 13: 978-1-4405-0595-9
eISBN 10: 1-4405-0742-2
eISBN 13: 978-1-4405-0742-7

Printed in the United States of America.

10 9 8 7 6 5 4 3 2 1

Library of Congress Cataloging-in-Publication Data
is available from the publisher.

DEDICATION

Thanks to our loyal friends, without you guys these would just be bad ideas—you made them unforgettable experiences. This book is dedicated to Johnny Schezuan, Catfish, Butterbean, Ski, Chief, Rojo Grande, Burt Destruction, Gwendo, the Skinny Ginger, Coco La Bell, Whitster, Bales, Garrison, McSquiggles, McLovin, Druding, Refried Burns, Flo, Critter, Swifty, Free-dog, Shan and Claire, Goose, Pusso, Flaherty, Slutricio, the Kirby Bros., and Zan.

CONTENTS

ACKNOWLEDGMENTS

We would like to thank our literary agent Hannah Brown Gordon (the Scottish Jew) for being the first person to believe in this project, our manager Matt Schuler, our editor Brendan O'Neill for bringing it all together, and Colleen Cunningham for a great design.

Lastly, we want to thank our parents: Mike, Mary Jo, Don, and M'Gee. You guys didn't know this at the time, but every fake I.D., drinking citation, call from the cops, and pick-up from the drunk-tank were all part of a master plan that led to this book being published. Every bad decision we ever made has now been validated. We're sorry for being shitheads from the age of fifteen, but hopefully the revenue from these ideas will help in cleaning your bedpans one day.

INTRODUCTION

This good book for great times is designed to teach you how to have more fun. The deal is simple: Use these ideas to throw kick-ass parties. Follow our lead and your social life will improve for all of eternity. For real.

The following advice is by far the most serious section of the book. Don't get all scared by the preachy lingo. Trust in your good book. We've put our moderately priced Catholic school educations to good use breaking down the elements of a great event. We present, The Art of the Party.

THE ART OF THE PARTY: 10 RULES FOR PARTY PLANNERS

1. People—Quality over Quantity

When a crowd becomes too large to manage, the quality of people can suffer. Throwing a huge shit show is fun, but you can almost always count on the following things to happen: losing money, cleaning up vomit, and two angry drunk guys bumping into each other. To avoid these common mistakes, we keep most of our guest lists around thirty to forty people. A small, well-organized party can create a level of synergy that is more intoxicating than the Popov vodka you are drinking. Invite fun people who are going to contribute. Judgmental partiers can ruin the mood. Find the ones that are excited to be doing something creative.

2. Be Respectful to Girls

When throwing a party, our goal is to have fun, not to get laid. You will be very successful as a party planner if you create fun environments where females feel safe. This can take time and patience, but will lead to groups of girls who come to every event. If someone in your circle is being disrespectful, ban him from the next party. Alcohol is going to lead to sexual situations. This does not mean that it will always happen, so don't force it. Combining groups of girls can also be difficult, so as a host, organize activities that break up groups of catty girls.

3. Keep an Even Ratio

When planning your event try to keep an even ratio of males and females. This will create a comfortable balance. When there is a shortage of girls, guys become over aggressive and try to monopolize female attention. When there is a shortage of guys, girls get bored quickly and want to move to a more stimulating environment like a club. When the ratio is even, people will comfortably mingle until they find someone interesting.

4. Themes and Costumes Are Key

Themes act as the creative hook that draws people to the event. Pick one that challenges partygoers to rise to the occasion. Themes encourage people to plan and/or shop for their outfit, adding to the overall experience.

If you follow these rules, you'll be able to create dozens of unforgettable experiences that will always trump the stories of those clubbing, bottle-service douche bags. That's the 5th Year guarantee.

The awkward hour of a typical party occurs when people begin to arrive. Costumes are the best icebreaker for strangers. It creates a feeling that even though you don't know everyone, you're all in this together. Suddenly, those spandex tights and leg warmers don't feel so uncomfortable. As the first drink starts to hit, you realize that you and everyone else at the party are in for a good night.

5. Send a Great Invitation

A well-written invitation is one of the most critical parts of a successful party. An invitation sets the tone and addresses the issues that can cause uncertainty. Tell the guests exactly what they are getting into with a description that includes the location, theme, transportation, level of intoxication, and a detailed timeline. You have to create such an enticing invitation that your friends will worry that if they skip this Red Wine/White Suit Party they will have to hear about how much fun it was for weeks.

Send invitations out at least a week in advance. After people have responded, it's time to start the preparty e-mail war. E-mail blast everyone coming and let the trash talking begin. Almost like you're speculating on an upcoming sporting event, call people out for previous lackluster performances and criticize their drinking abilities. This will get people fired up and will ensure their full commitment. After the event, start a post-party email battle that includes crowning the Most Valuable Partier as well as the Least Valuable Partier (The Turd Ferguson Award), and go over a list of other people's highs and lows.

6. Designate Roles to Partygoers

Not every partier wants to be the center of attention, but all guests do enjoy contributing. Designate roles for people that suit their personalities. This lightens your load and makes people feel like they have stock in the party. Put two or three guys in charge of alcohol. This means cost, quality, and quantity. Put a few girls on decorations because they will be more detailed than males. Appoint someone DJ and have him or her create iPod playlists. Sometimes shy people don't want to participate, so give them a task or job like photographer. Always have one person who acts as the cruise director, keeping everyone busy with drinking games and contests. As the host, you should always keep an eye out for newcomers. Sometimes it's very intimidating for newbies to come into a really close group of friends, so the host should make them feel welcome. Know your friends' skills and try to put them to use at every event.

7. Stay Active—Don't Let Alcohol Be the Center of Attention

If people are hovering around the booze, you've failed as a party planner. Alcohol is a much-needed social lubricant, but it is best used as an enhancer, not the primary form of entertainment. This can be avoided by having activities planned before the party begins. We've included a bunch of games that will keep the energy levels up. People should be so preoccupied that they're forced to rush over to refill their drinks before the next game starts. Learn these games. Memorize them. Always have one ready to get people rocking.

8. Be the Pace Car of Intoxication

As a host, you have to observe the level at which people are consuming drinks. Be the pace car. Don't let partiers get too far ahead or too far behind. Keeping people on the same level will fuel the fire of a great time.

9. Details Count

What you do to go above and beyond is what your guests will remember and talk about. As a party planner, you have to be willing to go the extra mile to make your event more of an experience. These can be little things like creating nametags for drinking games, posting tournament-style brackets for beer pong, and organizing large group photographs. These little things add up to something much bigger. When the question comes up of whether or not you should go and buy temporary tattoos for your Citizenship Party, always consider that it's always worth the extra effort.

10. Don't Go to the Party—Create the Party

Be in control of your social life. Instead of throwing the standard Naked Girls and Horny Dudes Party, plan something original that will create a long-lasting memory. Once you've done a few successful events, you will be able to start building a network of like-minded people. When you and your friends are out having fun, people will gravitate towards your group. Grab their e-mails and invite them to the next event. We truly believe in the statement, "If you're bored, you're boring."

HOW TO GET PEOPLE TO SHOW UP

As a party planner, you have to motivate people to come to events. This can be like pulling teeth. If you were asking them to come to a club opening for [insert anorexic celebrity's clothing line here], all you would have to do is mention the magical four-letter word: list. Then they would wait outside in a line for two hours. However, a creative theme can have the opposite effect and scare some people away.

Our parties require a little bit of user participation, which directly conflicts with people's laziness. The lamer party-goers will use any excuse not to come so you have to have a counterattack ready for each excuse.

Reason: Typical Girl says, "I don't want to come because I don't know what to wear."
Counterattack: In the invitation, include a detailed explanation of the theme and a list of possible costume ideas. This will give all the girls an acceptable spectrum of ideas to choose. Girls don't fear dressing up (that's their favorite part), they just fear being criticized by other girls for having the sluttiest costume. Treat a party like a film set. You are the director setting the scene.

Partygoers are like actors who have to understand the environment so they can improvise. All it takes is a little push in the right direction and girls will build on your ideas.

Reason: Lazy Partier says, "I don't want to come because it's easier to just go out to bars."

Counterattack: After the general invitation goes out, individually contact people. Never ask them to come as a favor. Frame the invite in a way that appeals to them personally and will be hard for them to turn down. Here are some examples:

- *Single Girls: Compare the two environments . . . "Look, you can go out to a nightclub where every guy there is just going to use you as a story to validate himself to his other homoerotic friends or you can come to our party where you might actually meet someone interesting."*
- *Single Guys: Hit them where it hurts—the wallet . . . "Option #1: Go to the bar and try to impress people you don't like by pretending you have money and buying rounds. Option #2: Take half of the money you would normally spend at a club and bring something fun to the party (breathalyzer, Slip 'N Slide, karaoke machine, extra costumes). This will guarantee that you will meet some new girls. Spend less, get more."*
- *Couples: Frame it in a way that gives them fun things to do together . . . "Hey, you two should come to our party this weekend. We need some more good people there. I know this vintage store where you can find a good couple's costume, and right around the corner there's a little restaurant that you two would love."*

Reason: Half-Asser says, "I might stop by for a little bit, but I have other plans."

Counterattack: The Half-Asser will never come in costume. So when you go to get your outfit, pick up a couple cheap accessories like glasses, wigs, moustaches, and extra vintage clothes. Have them available at the front door. The minute these people show up, throw something on them and whisk them into the party. Don't give them time to even consider leaving. Throw them right into the middle of a game or activity and introduce them to some new people. Before you know it, the Half-Asser will hit the four-drink tipping point and decide to stay.

PARTIES WE WON'T PUBLISH AND WHY

We cover a lot in this book, but there are some party ideas that we wouldn't touch with a ten-foot pole because they're used more than guidettes from Jersey. Here is a list of five party themes that you won't find inside . . .

The Toga Party

Yes, this is the Godfather of all theme parties and we do pay homage to its roots. Throwing a Toga Party is like playing speed quarters with wooden nickels. The game is the same, but the tools have gotten better. Improve on good ideas with new ideas. Throwing a Toga Party while on a pub crawl in Rome is something worthy of a Facebook post. Throwing a Toga Party in your basement with the football team is not. Stay away from the toga.

Anything with Pros, Bros, or Hos

Is this the best you can come up with while sitting in your frat-house bunk bed trying to rub a chub without waking up your roommate? Pros, Bros, and Hos parties are the most uncreative themes. The equation is simple. Think of two groups of people that are mildly similar and tack a "bro" or "ho" on the end. Presto! You have another shitty idea. Some examples:

- *Pimps and Hos*
- *CEOs and Business Hos*
- *GI Joes and Barbie Hos*
- *Gangsta Hos and Thugged-Out Bros*
- *Eskimos and Inuit Hos*
- *Surf Pros and Beach Hos*
- *Redneck Bros and Hick Hos*

White Trash Bash

Although its very fun to ridicule the culture of belt loops stowing Natural Light, nutrition based around Slim Jims, and pregnant teenagers—the White Trash Bash has been played out. Let the NASCAR lovers have their wife-beaters and overalls.

'80s Party

The '80s were home to some of the most visually offensive styles and fashions in history. A newly wealthy class of yuppies were obsessed with material possessions, power suits, and cocaine—which led to bad decisions and even worse fashion. The '80s theme party has become the go-to unoriginal party. Some people just don't want to see those days go. I guess they have too many limousines with hot tubs and helicopter landing pads parked in their marble driveways. Vary the theme. Throw an "I was addicted to coke in the '80s but now I'm broke and sober" party. Try not to repeat the same ol' thing.

The Anything But Clothes Party

This party is a cheap attempt to see boobies. It may work on Jumbo Jack-munching bar trollops, but are these the kind of people you want at your party? Is it worth a night spent with "Johnny Show-Me-Your-Beaver" and "Sally I'll-Show-You-My-Beaver-for-Some-Free-Beer?" The more creative the idea, the better the people. This party usually ends up with fifteen naked guys doing penis flops into the pool. No thanks.

GET STARTED

It's time to think outside the proverbial party box. We're here to guide you and give you ideas, but you have to put these ideas into action. A party's only as fun as you make it. Put in the effort and you'll be rewarded with a great time your friends won't soon forget.

> AS YOU'RE ICING THE KEG, HANGING UP THE DECORATIONS, OR GETTING A ROUND OF FLIP CUP STARTED, JUST REMEMBER OUR MOTTO: IF YOU'RE BORED, YOU'RE BORING.

ALL-AMERICAN DAY

Dust off that American flag, work on your John Wayne impersonation, buy as much domestic beer as possible, and get ready to have your patriotism rocked to its core. In the immortal words of *Always Sunny in Philadelphia*'s Charlie Kelly:

"I'm gonna rise up, I'm gonna kick a little ass, I'm gonna kick some ass in the U.S.A., gonna climb a mountain, gonna sew a flag, gonna fly on an eagle. I'm gonna kick some butt, I'm gonna drive a big truck, I'm gonna rule this world, I'm gonna kick some ass, I'm gonna rise up, I'm gonna kick a little ass. ROCK, FLAG and EAGLE!!"

THE SET-UP

Pick a public park, lakefront, or big yard to host this patriotic event. All-American Day is a series of games, costumes, and food, American style. Just like America's immigration policy, anyone can attend this event. Make sure the foreigners know the revised pledge of allegiance,

"I pledge allegiance to this party in the United States of America, and to my friends holding me up for this keg stand, one nation, under domestic beer, indivisible with porno and corn dogs for all."

GAME SUGGESTIONS

Keep the patriotism pumping by getting partygoers to participate in these games . . .

Phone a Family or Friend Ethnic Joke Competition

Ethnic jokes are as American as apple pie and baseball. Celebrate our melting pot by organizing this contest. Pick an even amount of people and create a playoff bracket (*www.printyourbracket.com*). Go through your cell phone contacts, call someone of your choice, put them on speakerphone and make them tell you their best ethnic joke. If your joke receives more votes than your competitor, you advance to the next round. Once a person is called they cannot be called again. Calling your own minority friends offers a huge advantage because they usually spout off a chestnut about their own race. Our friend José gave us this little gem: "Why do Mexicans eat tamales on Christmas? Because they're the only things they have to unwrap." May the person with the most racist friends win. Game on.

The Redneck Relay Race

Organize two teams of four and make sure you have the following items: dual track slip and slide, light beers, watermelons, beer bongs, corn dogs, and a body of water.

Leg 1: The first contestants must go down the slip and slide and finish a beer bong being held by their teammate.

Leg 2: Once your teammate finishes his beer bong, run over to the table and finish a whole corn dog. Use the corn dog stick like a baton and hand off to the third leg.

Leg 3: The second and third leg then have to do a two-man wheelbarrow walk to the anchors that are waiting by the body of water with watermelons.

Leg 4: The anchors have to swim across the designated area of the lake/pool with the watermelon (they float). Once they are back to the starting point, the

AMERICAN ATTIRE MUST BE STRICTLY ENFORCED. OFFER UP COSTUME IDEAS LIKE HULK HOGAN, HILLARY CLINTON, SEXY ABE LINCOLN, UNCLE SAM, DALLAS COWBOY CHEERLEADERS, OLD-SCHOOL NATIVE AMERICANS, MARK TWAIN, HOOTERS WAITRESS, HACKSAW JIM DUGAN, SEXY STATUE OF LIBERTY, OR DECKING YOURSELF OUT IN RED, WHITE, AND BLUE GEAR.

watermelon must be broken open on your head or a teammates head. The first team to finish eating it wins.

Civil War Re-enactment

You need two water balloon launchers for this. Have two teams of guys stand roughly seventy-five yards apart. One team is the Union, one team is the Confederacy. Make sure there are no kids nearby, and then using the launchers, take turns trying to pelt your friends with water balloons traveling at about fifty MPH. The one rule is the receiving team is not allowed to move. Take turns calibrating wind, velocity,

PLAYLIST

Classic rock is perfect for daytime debauchery:

"American Woman"
The Guess Who

"Dixieland Delight"
Alabama

"Born on the Bayou"
Creedence Clearwater Revival

"Money for Nothing"
Dire Straits

"Rollin' and Tumblin'"
Eric Clapton

"Tusk"
Fleetwood Mac

"Success"
Iggy Pop

"Living in America"
James Brown

"American Girl"
Tom Petty

"Jack and Diane"
John Mellencamp

"Live and Let Die"
Guns N' Roses

"Tush"
ZZ Top

"Mississippi Queen"
Mountain

"Funk No. 49"
James Gang

"Stranglehold"
Ted Nugent

"Call Me the Breeze"
Lynyrd Skynyrd

"I Just Want to Make Love to You"
Foghat

"Black Betty"
Ram Jam

"New York Groove"
Kiss

"Who Do You Love?"
George Thorogood

arch, and tension. There is nothing better then giving one of your best friends a purple welt with a direct hit. If you don't have launchers, stand fifty feet apart and just Nolan Ryan each other.

Communist Firing Squad

Nothing is more American than a Communist witchhunt à la Joseph McCarthy. Throughout the day, use mob mentality to pick on the least enthusiastic American. Proceed to label him or her a Communist, get everyone else on your side through the use of irrational arguments then make him or her finish a beer and face the water balloon firing squad. "That'll teach those pinko commie bastards to be more enthusiastic!" Then get your latest victim to pick someone else.

Cheeto Head!

Have two contestants put on a shower/swim cap. Cover the cap in a shaving cream afro. Have the two people wearing shower caps stand ten to fifteen feet away from their team. Each team has one minute to throw and stick as many Cheetos as they can on their teammates shower cap. The team with the most after one minute wins.

ALL-AMERICAN SLANG

DeNiro has logged thousands of hours doing method-acting research. He lived with steel workers to prepare for *Deer Hunter* and worked as a cabbie for three months to get ready for *Taxi Driver*. You can't even focus long enough to finish a 140-character Tweet. Luckily, we've done the research for you. After attending some redneck thong pulls, Juggalo wrestling matches, and small-town events like Ohio's Poultry Day, we've come up with a list of lines to help you fit right in at your All-American Day celebration.

"Listen up . . . when I woke up this morning I didn't put on my fuck-me shoes, I put on my fuck-you shoes!"

"Well I'll be damned, do you need to be introduced to the sheriff [*raise left hand*] and the mayor [*raise right hand*] of Fist City?"

"'Tough titty' said the kitty when the milk went dry." (Courtesy of our high school P.E. teacher)

"Back when men were men, we didn't drink Frappuccinos and surf the 'Net; we drank Schlitz and shoveled manure."

"I only came here to do two things, kick some ass and drink some beer. Looks like we're almost outta beer." (Courtesy of Clint from *Dazed and Confused*)

COSTUME YOU VERY MUCH

5thYear loves a good costume party. You'll notice in this book that most of the events are based around hilarious themes paired with embarrassing costume ideas. The foundation of a party is built on the strength of its theme, but it's the individuals at the party who dictate the energy in the room. What makes a party exceptional is the level of detail and involvement of the attendees; this can be measured in awesomeness of costumes.

The core of a party's success is in the individual costumes sported by your guests. The more detailed the costume, the more time and energy the guest put in to being at your party. They are invested in the event. And their attention to detail will be matched by their excitement and energy. The opposite is equally true. A theme party where guests show up unprepared and uninvolved is a failure. People who show up sans costume are saying they're not excited to be there, killing the energy. (Those who show up in a last-minute ensemble pulled together from last year's Halloween costume are equally lazy and unoriginal.) Their thought process is, "I'm not wearing a stupid costume. I'm just gonna show up, bang some chicks, and get fucked up." Remember that. And think about keeping those gaping douche holes off the next invite list.

Costumes create a feeling of party euphoria. When wearing a costume, a partygoer is saying to the world, "I don't care if I look stupid. I'm having an awesome fucking time." If you ever look at photos from a costume party you'll notice a major difference from regular non-costume party pictures. Look at those people in the non-costume ones. They're just a bunch of mopey-faced beanbags sitting around in turtlenecks trying not to look stupid. Now look at the costume ones. Those people are *actually* partying. They're smiling, hugging, dancing, laughing, and one hell of a time. After putting on a costume, you can stop worrying about what people think about you for a little while, and focus on the sweet dance moves you're going to bust. Putting on a costume enhances the party mentality.

Getting people excited to dress up is key to the success of your social gathering. As the host, make sure it's clear that if people show up un-costumed, they will be punished by whips and chains and a firing squad of scorn that isn't even held to the Rules of Ridicule.

Rules of Ridicule: The parameters of acceptability for torturing, pranking, chiefing, or verbally abusing your friends. Pretty much everything is fair game except for talking about sisters and mothers in any sort of sexual manner.

TRUE, WEARING A COSTUME CAN MAKE YOU LOOK STUPID. BUT WHEN YOU BRING TOGETHER GIRLS AND GUYS IN HILARIOUS COSTUMES, MIX IN SOME ALCOHOL, AND TIE IT ALL TOGETHER UNDER SOME THEME, THE PARTY IS JUST MORE FUN.

There is always one scaredy-pants douche in your circle of friends who will pretend that he didn't know it was a theme party. In ours it's a guy named Pat. (Sorry Pat, you should have tried harder.) Have backup costumes ready for lame-o's like him. As punishment, they will be made fun of and blacklisted from future events. The enemy must pay.

At the end of the day, a costume knocks down the social barriers people bring to parties. Nervous energy is destroyed when everyone is dressed up. When people decide to let their social guard down, they start to have fun. Similar to alcohol, a costume gets people loosened up and ready to rock. Your pictures are better, people make better friends, and people learn to let their tits out a little bit. It's a 5th Year fact.

AUSSIE RULES PARTY! OI! OI! OI!

Anyone who has ever met a group of Australians knows that they're the best drinking buddies. The women are just as crazy as the men, and neither sex can say no to alcohol-inspired adventures. The Aussie Rules Party uses the time-honored American tradition of stereotyping our friends from Down Under. (Crocodile Dundee accent on . . .) "This is guaranteed to pack a wallop for all you blokes and Sheilas. Prepare to get kicked in the teeth by a beaut of a time, you bloody ankle-biters!"

THE SET-UP

You should pick a scorcha of a day for The Aussie Rules Party. It'll make you feel like you're really in the outback. You should plan to have it somewhere that has a yard big enough for a walkabout and a lawn 'bout knee high on a grasshopper.

The Games

Here are some Down Under drinking games to help you down some grog.

Trugo Tourney: Trugo is a game that was invented by rail workers in Melbourne, Australia. We've taken the basic elements and modified it into a dodgier version of beer pong. All that is needed is a big lawn, a croquet mallet, a hockey puck, and a bunch of canned beers. Setup two pyramids of six beers each (three in the back, two in the middle, one in front) roughly twenty-five feet apart. Each team of two has twenty-four tries to knock over all six of the opposing team's cans by standing up the hockey puck and striking it with the mallet so it rolls on its side into the cans. The catch: You have to face away from the cans, bend over, and swing the mallet through your legs. The first team to knock over all the cans wins. If the cans haven't been knocked over after each team gets twenty-four turns, the team with the most cans knocked down wins. (Losers have to finish the remaining beers still standing.) Set up a bracket just like you would for beer pong.

DRESS THE PART

For the Blokes:

Rugby Players (scrumcaps, jerseys, and short black rugby shorts)

Aussie Surfer Party Boys (Google "Corey Delaney")

Steve Irwin (either tasteful, or South Park-style)

Crocodile Dundee (any character from *Dundee*, including Donk)

For the Sheilas:

Koala Bears (gray mouse ears with black paint on your nose)

Kangaroos (short brown shorts, a big tail, and black paint on your nose)

Terri Irwin (khaki shorts and a khaki shirt like her late husband, Steve)

Aborigines (red bathing suits, spears, and decorative white body paint)

THIS PARTY IS DEDICATED TO THE AUSTRALIAN TWINS WE MET (ONE OF WHOM HAD ON A CAST FROM PUNCHING THE OTHER ONE) WHO TOLD US THEY USED TO GET DRUNK AND SHIT OFF THE ROOF WHILE THE OTHER TRIED TO CATCH IT IN A POT BELOW. GET ONYA MATE!

Trugo Tourney Team Names:

- *The Dundeezy's*
- *The Keith Ledgers*
- *The Blanchett Bombers*
- *The Dingos That Ate Your Baby*
- *The Elle McFearsomes*
- *The Jack Hugemans*
- *Nicole Kidman's Nipples*
- *Gibson's Lethal Weapons*
- *The Romper Stompers*
- *Bana's Buttholes*

The Champagne Scrum: Start by shaking up a few bottles of cheap champagne (Cook's or André). Then have the whole party stand about ten feet in front of you, while you open the bottle and shoot the cork into the air. Whoever comes out of the scrum with the cork gets to pick four people to finish the bottle. The winner also picks the order in which the four will drink; once one person breaks the lip-to-bottle seal, he has to pass the champagne to the next person. If the fourth person can't finish the bottle, he or she has to pour the remaining bubbly over their head. Repeat game until party is rocking.

Thunder from Down Under Dance-off: Everyone knows about the Thunder from Down Under, the male strip show from Oz. Sit five willing girls down in chairs and have five male contestants volunteer to give them lap dances. Speakers up. It's time for Australia's greatest export—blast ACDC's "Dirty Deeds Done Dirt Cheap." Let the male strippers embarrass themselves for a few minutes and use the crowd's applause to pick a winner.

The Crocodile Mile: Run two Slip 'N Slides side by side, with a beer in between them at the end. Match up partygoers and have them race against one another. Each racer gets an inflatable crocodile and a running head start. The first person to slide down the course on their croc and grab the beer wins the heat.

AWKWARD PARTY

We've all done or said something at a party that has led to an awkward silence, like the kind that follows your gay joke—when you're seated next to the gay guy—or you asking a woman how far along in her pregnancy she is only to find out she's just packed on some holiday pounds. All you can really do at that point is put your foot in your mouth and enjoy the awkwardness. But just because it's awkward, doesn't mean it's not hilarious.

The Awkward Party invites uncomfortable comments and embarrassing moments into one night of inappropriate behavior. For once, you can say all of those taboo thoughts out loud, and everyone will laugh. (We hope.)

THE SET-UP

Do the opposite of what you would normally do to prepare for guests. Instead of making sure the bathrooms are stocked with plenty of soap, hand towels, and toilet paper, get rid of all of those luxuries and let your guests awkwardly search for something else to clean up with. "Um . . . I know this is awkward, but I just took a huge dump and you didn't have any toilet paper . . . so I had to wipe with my own sock. Now it's clogged."

> IF YOU HAVE THE NECESSARY TOOLS, TAKE THE BATHROOM DOOR DOWN, AND MAKE IT REAL AWKWARD FOR YOUR PARTY GUESTS.

Yes, things will get weird, and they should. It's an awkward party. No biggie if the milk is a little rotten, or if there is a dead fly in the bowl of jungle juice. Encourage it. Put out food that is typically not served at parties. Some things I would never want to touch at a party—so they should definitely be served at yours—include:

- *Glasses of milk*
- *Gefilte fish*
- *Jell-O molds*
- *Shared dipping sauces*
- *Caramel apples*
- *Hardboiled eggs*
- *Pudding*
- *Cottage cheese*
- *Asparagus*

And be sure to set the mood accordingly. Leave some porno magazines out on the coffee table and in the bathrooms. When new people show up, make sure the music is off and everyone just stares at each other in silence. This'll be really awkward. Perfect. Once everyone has arrived, start the inappropriate conversations. Be sure to talk about religion and politics. This always gets people feeling a little uneasy. Say you don't believe in God, and that you don't think we should have to support people on welfare. And there's no way out. "Um . . . this is awkward, where's the bathroom?" They'll soon find out that there is no door. They just have to accept the awkwardness.

Keep the Awkward Coming

Here are some awkward things to make sure the awkwardness is at eleven:

Leave your fly unzipped

Have toilet paper stuck to your shoe

Keep something in your teeth

Leave un-popped white heads on your face

Smell like B.O.

Wear way too much Stetson cologne

Tuck your underwear into your skirt

Have some serious dandruff

Talk way too loud

Laugh way too much

Never laugh

Wear sunglasses inside

Tell people they're really pretty and then smell them

Fart and don't walk away

Eat all the food without sharing

Don't clean up after yourself

Criticize people's appearances

Talk about how you have sex

Talk about your relationship issues

Eat with your mouth open

One-up everyone

Interrupt everyone

Touch your junk while people are telling stories

Ask people to take pictures of you, alone

Ask people if they have ever had an STD, when they say "No," respond, "Lucky" and walk away

Be a close-talker

Freeze and stare in the middle of conversation

Show off your dance moves

Place a bed in your living room

The more awkward, the better. Make sure almost everyone knows that you're throwing an awkward party. Don't tell a few of the people you invite about the theme, so they are really confused, and it's ultra awkward. To the max.

STAY ENTERTAINED

Put all participants names on a "Hello My Name Is" sticker and take turns pulling them out of a hat. Once you slap on your chosen nametag, you have to act like that person. Copy your friend's mannerisms, sayings, speech, and even start speaking in first person while dishing out fun facts about "yourself." Be careful not to go *too* far because someone in that room will be playing you. Watch and laugh as the intoxication levels rise and the impersonations get ruthless. Talk about awkward.

Warning: This drinking game can get ugly. This is best played with a group of friends that know each other well.

PLAYLIST

Keep your guests uneasy by constantly switching tempos and genres.

"I'd Do Anything for Love"
Meat Loaf

"Gettin' Jiggy Wit It"
Will Smith

"Blow Job Betty"
Too Short

"Mambo Number 5"
Lou Bega

"Ass and Titties"
Three Six Mafia

"Hanging Tough"
New Kids on the Block

"Make Em' Say Uhh!"
Master P

"Barbie Girl"
Aqua

"Real Muthaphuckkin G's"
Easy E

"Look at this Photograph"
Nickelback

"Break Stuff"
Limp Bizkit

"Get Munked"
Alvin and the Chipmunks

"Who Let the Dogs Out"
Baha Men (I got thrown out of the dorms for putting this song on repeat in someone else's room, bolting the door from the inside, and jumping out the second story window. It played for over an hour.)

BEACH BUNKER BONANZA

Fire in the hole! Water balloons are whizzing by your head at fifty MPH, *but you don't care . . . you are on a mission . . . a mission for beer. Exit your bunker, charge the battlefield, and try not to get killed. It's a war zone out there.*

The Beach Bunker Bonanza is the perfect combination of warm weather and a mass consumption of the performance dehancing drug, light beer. Camouflage gear, helmets, and war paint is encouraged.

THE SET-UP

The field of play is a beach, or any sandy area where you can dig a bunker. Organize your friends in teams of three to four people. Build your bunker with your team. A bunker is a hole in the ground that is used as a shelter from enemy fire. Bunkers are built around the central keg. The keg has its own bunker. Bunkers cannot be built closer than thirty yards to the keg. That space is no-man's land and when inside, you become an open target.

The object of the game is to get to the keg, fill up your beer, and get back to your bunker without getting decimated by an onslaught of enemy fire. If you do get hit, your beer becomes property of the bunker that nailed you. March to the enemy bunker; fill up everyone's cups, and head back to your bunker empty-handed. Your team will be very disappointed with your futile efforts.

Try always having a steady supply of beer to ration for your bunkmates. Take turns filling up the pitcher . . . be smart, run hard, and don't be a hero . . . you'll get destroyed every time.

Every thirty minutes, one member from each team is rotated to a different bunker. This will keep the excitement moving and allow for more interaction. Newcomers always run first. It's like Mr. Payne said in *Dazed and Confused*, "Fifty of you are leaving on a mission. Twenty-five of you ain't coming back."

Team Names That Scream Binge Drinking

- *Weapons of Mass Consumption*
- *The Bomb Jovis*
- *The Camo-Jockeys*
- *The BeerZookas*
- *The Boozageddons*
- *The Destroya-saurases*
- *The Patriot Racks*
- *The Missile Tits*
- *The Bunker Busters*
- *The Camo-Toes*

After you have played Beach Bunker, you can organize some other great open-air activities: Minefield (see the Vietnam Vet Party), Beersbee (see Outdoor Concert), or KanJam.

KAN JAM TOURNEY

Beer pong is a little too tame to follow up the Bunker raid. You need another excuse to drink an eighteen-pack. Salvation lies in a new game sweeping America and it's called Kan Jam. Visit *www.Kanjam.com* to order your set today (only $34.99 or in college economics, dos thirty-packs). Here's the general concept behind the game from *www.Kanjam.com*:

- Kan Jam is played with one Frisbee and two bucket-shaped goals. Kan Jam is played with two teams of two.
- The goals are placed fifty feet apart.
- Teams take turns throwing the Frisbee to their teammate while he/she tries to use their hands to deflect the Frisbee into the bucket.
- The objective of the game is to score 21 points.

  Dinger (one point): If a player redirects a throw and it hits the container but does not go in.

  Deuce (two points): The thrower directly hits the container without the help of his teammate.

  Bucket (three points): The deflector hits the thrown Frisbee directly into the bucket.

- Each container has a Frisbee-sized slot in the front. If a player throws it through the slot, it is an instant win.

OVER THE TOP

Here are a few ideas on how to take the game to the next level:

Make the teams co-ed: Nothing is worse than two obnoxious dude-bros dominating a competition.

Team names: Each team name should be a '90s jam band.

Tie-dye shirts and colored bandanas are required: Frisbee is associated with the Grunge hippies of the '90s, so dress accordingly: Birkenstocks, tinted glasses, headbands, jam-band tee shirts, flannel grunge, hemp jewelry, and the combat boots/denim shorts combo. Watch *PCU* (an underrated classic) for inspiration.

Buy a big poster board: Keep track of wins and losses.

Buy some kind of hippie trophy for the winning team: lava lamp, incense holder, baja hoodies, mushroom candles, or a Bob Marley poster.

Note: *www.Kanjam.com* has a printable PDF of all the general rules and scoring. Have these handy for your tournament or else!

bEASTER EGG HUNT

It's simple. Substitute the plastic eggs with decorated cans of Milwaukee's Best.

THE SET-UP

bEaster is held one Sunday after the traditional zombie Jesus day they call Easter. Supplies are cheap as dog poop the week after Easter, so head to your local drugstore and stock up on baskets, Cadbury Eggs, Peeps, bunny ears, cardboard decorations, and paint.

Have your friends come over Sunday morning, make some mimosas, and start decorating the cans. The cans should be decorated with one color each. The colors correspond to points based on the difficulty of the can's hiding place. Cram all the contestants in one bathroom while the bEaster bunny (the host) then hides all of the colored cans. Make the bathroom guests finish a thirty-pack of light beer before they can start the search for eggs.

Yellow: 1 point. *Examples:* underneath planters, up in trees, between couch cushions

Blue: 2 points. *Examples:* deep inside cabinets, inside of rain gutters, duct-taped underneath tables

Pink: 3 points. *Examples:* inside the toilet tank, covered in dog poop, buried in the backyard

Keep them on their toes and hide one or two green cans. Let them drink the beers first and then tell them greens are not worth any points.

The bEaster Egg Hunt Rules

1. Break into teams of two. Each team must have a basket and an Easter-themed team name.
2. When a team finds a beer, they have to run back to their basket to finish it. All baskets are placed on a judge's table. Once the beer is finished, they can continue to hunt for more cans.
3. The team with the most points at the end of fifteen minutes is declared the winner.

AFTER THE HUNT

Don't let the hunt be the pinnacle of the day. Keep the Easter spirit (buzz) going with a Peep Eating Competition. Contestants sit at a table and take turns rolling a dice. Contestants tap out when they can't eat any more. The last man standing wins.

- ⚀ Eat a Peep
- ⚁ Make another player eat a Peep
- ⚂ Eat two Peeps
- ⚃ Make another player eat two Peeps
- ⚄ Finish your bEaster can
- ⚅ Eat a Cadbury Egg (the worst)

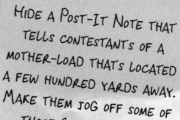

HIDE A POST-IT NOTE THAT TELLS CONTESTANTS OF A MOTHER-LOAD THAT'S LOCATED A FEW HUNDRED YARDS AWAY. MAKE THEM JOG OFF SOME OF THOSE CADBURY EGGS.

BEER OLYMPICS

Everything we know about Greek mythology comes from watching epic movies; so it's safe to assume Greeks are made up of curly locks, Orlando Bloom pube-staches, Brad Pitt six packs, and olive skinned, big-boob goddesses that were so hot they scared the men into gaydom. That's a fact.*

Thanks to the homoerotic oil rubbers that created the Olympics, we were able to design our own Olympiad based around the decimation of light beer by the thousands. Our Olympic forefathers have inspired us to rise up from the catacombs of inebriation and carry on the tradition that is "The Beer Olympics." Nations compete in the name of mindless jollification to earn the title of "Champions of the Golden Nectar of the Gods."

*All "facts" are pulled out of the 5th Year ass-crack of information technology.

THE SET-UP

Beer Olympics is day drinking event consisting of teams of four competing in five drinking events:

- *Beer Pong*
- *Speed Quarters*
- *Flip Cup*
- *Anchorman*
- *Beer Darts*

Detailed explanations of the games follow. Each game has a point system for first, second, and third. Buy poster board and make the brackets for the events.

EACH TEAM SHOULD COME UP WITH ITS OWN NAME THAT IS CLOSELY ASSOCIATED WITH A GEOGRAPHICAL PLACE: BEERUIT, BEERZENSTEIN, BEERSTANBUL, BEERJINGS, BEERHANNESBURG, BEERLIN, BEERBODIA, BEERMUDA, RUSKY BRUSKIES, SAUDI BEERABIA, BEERU, PAPUA NEW BEERS, BEERAGUAY, OR BEERGLADESH.

The Rules

1. Each team is made up of two guys and two girls.
2. In the beer pong event, each team has one coed squad on both the Western and Eastern brackets. The rest of the events are played with entire team.
3. If a team places first in an event they were awarded three points, second is two points, and third is one point.
4. At the end of all the games, the top four teams advanced to the final beer pong bracket, where the first and fourth seed played the winner of the second and third seed in the championship game. Do this so every team has a chance to sneak into the final beer bong bracket. That way a dark horse always has a shot to win gold.
5. If any team has members that can't go on, they are automatically disqualified. Endurance becomes a huge factor in winning the competition.

Make sure you have enough food and alcohol to last the whole day. Tell everyone on the e-vite to bring a thirty-pack and a tray of food. The food is important; you don't want people leaving because they get hungry. If you're hosting, you should have the following on hand: ping pong balls (get a bunch), metal darts, poster board, and Sharpies.

Greet everyone as they come in. You might even want to stage your own Opening Ceremonies parade. Then once everyone has arrived, stick your finger up your butt and smell it (it's a Greek thing) and let the games begin!

THE GAMES

Event #1: Anchorman. This game requires one beer pitcher, eight quarters (one for each player), and two teams of four people. Each team lines up on one side of a table and takes turns trying to bounce a quarter into a full pitcher. Genius! The team that sinks all of their quarters first wins. When one person is left struggling to make their quarter, we recommend screaming at them and making very offensive personal comments about their childhood. The pressure is on.

Once a team has all of their quarters in the pitcher, they win. The winning team gets to decide the drinking order for the losing team by picking the first, second, third, and anchorman. Each losing player drinks as much as he can, but as soon as his lips leave the pitcher they have to pass it to the next teammate. The anchorman must finish what is left, or dump the pitcher over his head.

Event #2: Beer Bong or Beirut. If you don't know how to play this game, you have no business reading this book and should Google image search "tubgirl."

Event #3: Speed Quarters. SQ is played around a circular table with alternating players from both teams standing

next to each other. The game is played with coffee mugs and quarters and the purpose is to catch up with the cup in front of you. The cups always move clockwise and if you sink the quarter on the first try, you can pass it to anyone on the table. Play this game to five eliminations.

Event #4: Beer Darts. YouTube some Ocho Cinco endzone dances because this game demands some creative celebrations. The dartboard is set up using nine cans of beer on the ground. Eight of the cans should be placed down horizontally in an octagon formation. The ninth beer should be vertical in the middle of the octagon, acting as the bull's eye.

The Rules

1. Each game is played to twenty-five points.
2. Each team must have set a lineup.
3. A rope is hung approximately eight feet high halfway in front of the throwers. All darts must go over this rope for the points to count.

The points: one point for outside the circle touching can, two points for inside the circle not touching anything, three points for a punctured horizontal can, and ten points for a punctured vertical bull's eye can. Puncturing a can is a joyous occasion. While the geyser of beer shoots into the air, bust out your best "Icky shuffle." The throwing team then hands the punctured beer to any opponent and they must finish it.

Event #5: Survivor Flip Cup. Have two teams line up on opposite sides of the table. Use red plastic cups and fill them up about a quarter of the way. Make sure everyone has the same amount, no cheaters. Start with the ends, and have opposing players "cheers" each other, tap their cup to the table, then chug. After the beer is done, the player must flip his cup from upright position to upside down position. Once he lands this flip, the next person can start chugging. So forth and so on, you should fucking know how to play this.

Now for the "Survivor" part. After each round, one player gets voted off of each team by the opposing team. The best players are usually voted off first making the final rounds the least experienced drinkers. The pressure is on!

BLOODS AND CRIPS AIRSOFT WAR

No matter how exciting your life may be, it's natural to settle into a weekly routine. The Bloods and Crips Airsoft War is a perfect way to liven up the monotony of Monday through Friday. Think about it: Ever gone to the laundromat strapped? Or been shot in the head while doing calf raises at the gym? Didn't think so. But doesn't it sound exciting?

THE SET-UP

This is a weeklong event you can organize with two teams of five to ten people. Half your friends are Bloods and half are Crips. Every gang member then goes to the local sporting goods store and buys their heat (clear Airsoft pistols). Make it a rule that you can only buy the clear plastic pistols. There are too many crazy stories about kids almost getting shot by cops who thought they were carrying real guns. Be safe and get the clear ones.

Once the teams are settled and the weapons have been purchased, the competition begins on Monday morning at 7 A.M. Play as if it were a real gang war.

The Rules

1. If you get shot you are out of the game.
2. The gang with the most players alive by Friday night (5 P.M.) wins the turf war.
3. The losing gang must host a party (at their house) for the winners.

This event will make your boring work week much more exciting because you'll be watching your back at all times. There will be drive-by attempts and full-fledged shootouts. However, both teams will soon realize that the most effective way to win this war is patient assassinations. Information suddenly becomes very important to the success of your kills. Most roommates, girlfriends, or family members will inadvertently "narc" on their loved ones at some point. Use that information to take down the target.

Your life will become a nervous wreck, coming home thinking someone might be in your house waiting to take you out. Some gang members might even arm their coworkers in case of an ambush at work. You can trust no one.

Come Friday afternoon at 5 P.M. the turf war ends and it's time to party.

THE BONG HIT OLYMPICS

Have you ever been so high that you thought your eyes could shoot lasers at the guy making your six-foot bologna and bacon ranch sub? No? Then we encourage you to have this party; it's a good one.

We aren't encouraging people to do drugs; we're just giving people suggestions so if they do decide to do drugs, they have some good activities to keep them busy. Everyone knows about the harmful effects of smoking marijuana. Mostly just laziness. The Bong Hit Olympics (BHO) actually promotes activity towards one of society's most inactive participants. Instead of watching *Family Guy* reruns and not showering, organize the Bong Hit Olympics in your own backyard.

THE SET-UP

Organize this event on a Saturday or Sunday afternoon with about twelve to fifteen friends. Split up into teams of three and designate a referee (the friend that doesn't smoke weed because he gets too paranoid).

An argument between a group of stoned kids can take hours, maybe even days. Make sure you have an impartial judge that can keep the pace moving forward. You don't want something as complicated as a Cheetos vs. Doritos debate to get in the way of an awesome afternoon.

The Rules

1. Each win is one point.
2. The team with the most points at the end of all the games is deemed winner.
3. Keep it simple for the pot-icipants. The weed river of random thoughts is limiting their ability to comprehend anything above a fourth grade level.

TEN GAMES FOR THE BONG HIT OLYMPICS

The Jigsaw Puzzle

Have the host/referee buy three of the same one hundred piece jigsaw puzzles. First team to finish their puzzle wins.

P.O.T.

A shortened version of the backyard basketball game "H.O.R.S.E.," only for less-coordinated participants. The team with the last player in wins.

Dorito Breath

The first team to finish a large bag of Doritos wins.

Thursday the 12th

Each team gets ten minutes to come up with the best horror movie premise. Each movie must have a plot, logline, protagonist, and antagonist. The referee will listen to each team pitch their movie and pick a winner.

Grilled Cheese Cook-Off (Lunch Competition)

Each team is allowed to add two nonmeat ingredients (from the kitchen) to a grilled cheese sandwich. The referee will taste test and award a point for the best combination.

Cotton Mouth Challenge

Each team is given one sleeve of Saltine crackers (thirty-eight) and they have to eat as many as they can without drinking water. The team that eats the most wins.

Customer Service Call

One player from each team is nominated to try to keep a retail employee (Hollister, Abercrombie & Fitch, or American Eagle) on the phone as long as possible. The player cannot tell them it's a game, being on hold does not count, and all calls are done on the cell phone speaker. The referee will use a stopwatch to declare a winner. Stores cannot be called twice in a row.

The Smiley Game

All contestants sit across from each other at a dinner table. The objective is to make your opponents laugh first. Players can make faces or movements but cannot make any noise. The team with the last man to laugh wins.

Channel Surfing

The referee holds the remote control and cycles through the first seventy channels of television. The first team to yell out the name of the television show, movie, or product (for commercials) wins a point. The team with the most points after seventy channels wins the competition.

Build a Bong

Each team gets twenty minutes to try and build a workable bong with household items. Referee should judge on two categories: creativity and usability.

THE BOOGIE NIGHTS POOL PARTY

You've got a guy with a twelve-inch ding dong, a child molesting financier, a veteran porn star who wants to be a magician, a girl who wears her roller skates during sex, and a whole bunch of amphetamines, cocaine, and recording tapes that hold magic. This is the reason that anything involving the '70s should be considered a Boogie Nights Party.

THE SET-UP

Nothing says, "Butter in your ass and lollypops in your mouth" better than a '70s pool party based on the movie *Boogie Nights*. Find the animated cover to the movie and copy it onto your invitations. It's time to boogie.

Get your friends to dress up as characters from the movie or come up with your own fictitious '70s porn star names. Make sure you have an ample supply of "Hello My Name Is" nametags for people's fake porn names. If people come unprepared (they always do), make one up for them. You can use the porn star name generator of mixing your:

- *middle name*
- *street name*
- *pet's name*

If that doesn't satisfy your raunchiness, then you can adopt one of our suggestions. Make sure to include the name of the actor/actress and his/her most recent film.

BOOGIE NIGHTS CHARACTERS

Dirk Diggler	Scotty J.
Jack Horner	Little Bill
Reed Rothchild	Todd Parker
Amber Waves	Jessie St. Vincent
Rollergirl	The Colonel
Buck Swope	Floyd Gondolli
T.T. Rodriguez	Becky Barnett

FUN PORN-STAR NAMES

Hugh G. Rection	April Flowers
Harry Balsagna	Candy Manson
Pacheco Suave	Harley Slickbooty
Little Oral Annie	Tara Hard
Ben Dover	Harry Nastee
Wendy Whoppers	General Jiggles
Mike Hunt	Don Cucumber
Chris Peacock	Jenna Asstronut
Flick Shagwell	Dick Dangle
Cherry Poppins	Johnny Jammer
B.B. Guns	Kinky Strokum
Sindee Cox	Rambone
Summer Cummings	
Hardon Ron	
B.J. Darkhole	

BROWN BAG SURPRISE PARTY

As you open your brown paper bag, you think, what the hell am I going to do with a roll of duct tape, cellophane wrap, and pink fishnet stockings? You have to wear that outfit, with no complaints, for the rest of the night. Get ready for catcalls, because you'll be heading to your nearest dive bar for dancing and debauchery.

THE SET-UP

Use a friend's house as home base to start the party. This is where you will be exchanging the brown bags. Make sure the house is walking distance from a dive bar (preferably one that allows groups of homeless-looking partygoers to have some "creative drinking space"). Going out in public sounds scary. Honestly, this is the best part of the night. Expect some catcalls from cowboys, some "What in the hell" from grandpas, and a few "Look at those fairies" from douchebags. At the end of the day, you are having way more fun than they are. Even Grandpa.

Hit up your local thrift stores, 99 Cent Stores, or Goodwills to find the most disgusting, ridiculous, and mismatched outfit. The costume must include a top and bottom. Girls shop for girls. Guys shop for guys. Sizes are never a perfect fit, so buy something stretchy.

Show up to the party wearing something basic. Everyone should bring their costume in a brown grocery bag, clearly labeled with their name written on the outside of the bag. Have a few drinks and let everyone get loosened up before you start handing out gag-balls and adult diapers.

Make a list of everyone's name at the party. If you're the host, buy a couple extra costumes in case you get the straggler who didn't get the instructions. Put everyone's name into a hat and then take turns drawing. You will wear the brown bag costume brought by that person.

Make sure to have a camera handy when people open their bags. The reactions are priceless. Watching someone's face when they pull out a roll of duct tape and plastic wrap makes this party worth every minute.

Everyone must wear their selected outfit . . . no exceptions. If you have a friend who is too embarrassed, you might want to reevaluate your friendship with that douche hole . . . "Hmm . . . let me just open my bag here. Okay, a pair of long underwear, rain boots, a fur trapper hat, and a pair of assless chaps. I think I need another beer."

THE MORE ACCESSORIZES THE BETTER (WIGS, JEWELRY, HATS), BUT THE SPENDING LIMIT SHOULD BE CAPPED AT $30 (YOU CAN GET AWAY WITH SPENDING $10). THE POINT OF THIS PARTY IS TO FIND THE WORST POSSIBLE COSTUMES FOR YOUR FRIENDS TO WEAR IN PUBLIC. BE RUTHLESS. PICK SOMETHING THAT YOU WOULD ONLY WEAR IF YOU WERE SUDDENLY NAKED IN DOWNTOWN MANHATTAN.

BYOB (BE YOUR OWN BOOZE) COSTUME PARTY

José Cuervo is pissing in your mom's rose bush, Captain Morgan just steam-poohed the only bathroom in the house (fucking pirates), Stoli and V8 are making out on the couch, and Jägermeister won't stop puking in the sink. Who invited Peppermint Schnapps? Damn it!

THE SET-UP

Each person or couple coming to the party is responsible for one bottle of alcohol or case of beer and the mixers required for their drink. And they have to dress in accordance with the brand of alcohol. The host should provide additional mixers, fresh fruit, blenders, and bar supplies.

Depending on the size of the party, you can go about the sharing two different ways. If you're planning a packed-house rager, it's probably best to just set up some tables and have partygoers pour their drinks into sampler cups. That way everyone can mingle and try what everyone else brought. But if you're going for a more intimate dinner-party type setting, you should have each partygoer prepare a quick history of the drink they brought to share. Who says parties can't be educational?

Top Ten Phrases to Replace "Let's Get Drunk!"

1. "Let's get weird!"
2. "Take it to the abyss!"
3. "Turn up the fun meter!"
4. "Do work!"
5. "Stop! Get Hammered time!"
6. "Go big or go home!"
7. "Time to ride Smash Mountain!"
8. "Let's get fucking wasted!"
9. "Let's visit the future!"
10. "I am pre-emptively apologizing for my actions."

BEER COSTUMES

Fosters
Outback attire

Sam Adams
Colonial attire

St. Pauli's Girl
sexy beer-wench costume

Labatts
Canadian hockey players missing teeth

Steinlager
Hobbits or rugby players

Asahi
ninja costumes

Red Stripe
Rastafari gear

Pabst
skinny jean hipsters

You Are What You Drink

BOOZE	DRINK	INGREDIENTS	COSTUME
Alizé	Pink Pussy Slam (shooter)	Alizé, pineapple juice, and splash of grenadine	Super-cool, thug-life gangsta rapper like Chamillionaire
Bacardi Rum	Orangesicle (cocktail)	Bacardi Rum, cream, and orange juice	Bermuda tourist in tropical island attire
Bailey's Irish Cream	Oatmeal Cookie (shooter)	Bailey's, butterscotch schnapps, and a dash of cinnamon	St. Patrick's Day attire
Beefeater Gin	The Bumble Bee (cocktail)	Gin, crushed ice, lemon juice, and honey	English Royalty (red capes, crowns, and scepters)
Captain Morgan	The Blackbeard (cocktail)	Captain Morgan's, Coke, and root beer schnapps	Pirate attire
Dewar's Scotch	Dr. Dewar's (cocktail)	Dewar's and Dr. Pepper	*Braveheart* face paint and kilts
José Cuervo	Tequila Poppers (shooter)	One part tequila, one part 7Up (put hand over the shot glass; slam it on the table; drink while bubbling)	Spring Break party-starter with a sombrero and whistle (blow your whistle, feed people shots, and shake their heads as they drink)
Malibu Rum	Surfers on Acid (shooter)	Jägermeister, Malibu rum, and pineapple juice	Hollywood Celebrities in Malibu beach attire
Southern Comfort	Redneck Cocktail (cocktail)	Southern Comfort and Mountain Dew	Hillbillies (overalls, blacked-out teeth, and fake tattoos)
Stolichnaya Vodka	Siberian Sunrise (blended)	Stoli vodka, grapefruit juice, and triple sec	Russian fur hats, military attire, and toy guns

CAFE PRESS PUB CRAWL

CafePress.com is a great resource for finding hilarious and offensive tee shirts. This makes it a great place to construct the perfect shirt that nobody would ever want to wear in public. Go onto the site, and start a search for "funny shirts" or just make your own. This party only works if everyone brings shirts. Yes, you have to order and pay for the shirts . . . it's way better than an overdesigned tiger bead shirt, we promise. All pub crawlers have to bring their shirt in a paper bag. The shirt you order will be worn by a friend, so find the right combination of ruthless and funny.

THE SET-UP

Have everyone meet at the first bar. Put the girls' shirts and guys' shirts in different piles on the pool table. Let everyone get a drink and then take turns randomly picking a bag. You have to wear the shirt you pick for the pub crawl. If you catch someone with his or her shirt off, make him buy you a drink. The host needs to have a series of bars picked out for the crawl. Throw on your shirts, and get that party moving.

SHIRT IDEAS FOR GUYS

Trophy Husband

Ranch Dressing Is Good

Gaydar Activate!

Meat Is Murder. Tasty. Tasty. Murder.

Ask Me About My Explosive Diarrhea

Lick Me Where I Pee

Back Off I'm Gonna Fart

Oedipus: The Original Mother Fucker

Yes! I Have Man-Boobs

I'm Not Gay But My Boyfriend Is

Hung Like a 5-Year-Old

There's Nothing Like a Fart That Vibrates Your Balls

Club Sandwiches Not Seals

I Love Foreskin

2QT2BSTR8

I Eat Pussy Like a Fat Kid Eats Cake

I Am Not Addicted to Cocaine. I Just Like How It Smells.

SHIRT IDEAS FOR GIRLS

Sperm Dumpster

Fluffer

I Blow for Bling

Girls Don't Poop

I'm So Pretty I Fart Pixie Dust

Got Fupa?

Idaho? No. Udaho!

Would It Help If I Bounce?

I Pooped Today!

Once You Go Persian There's No Better Version

I'm a Virgin: This Is a Very Old Shirt

I Interned Under President Clinton and All I Got Was This Stain on My Clothes

MILF: It Does a Body Good.

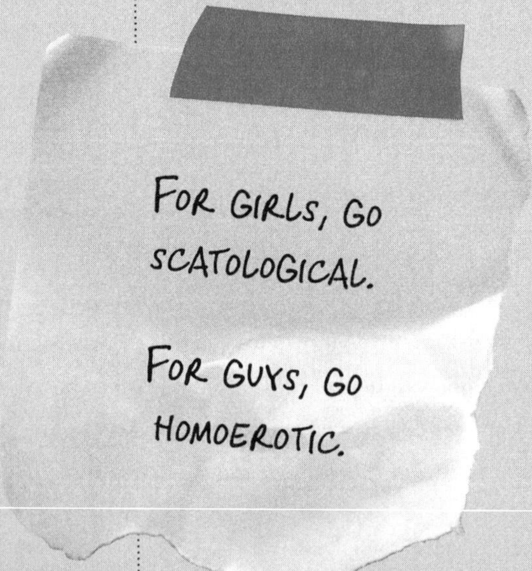
FOR GIRLS, GO SCATOLOGICAL.
FOR GUYS, GO HOMOEROTIC.

Here's a pre-pub crawl text message from Boring, Blonde, Ex-Sorority Post-Grad to her friend, Faux-hawked Sales Douche:

OMG! so xcited 4 ur golf pro pubcrawl. gr8 idea! gonna get cray cray!! TTYL

Don't be like these uninspired fucktards. Plan one of these original pub crawls that will attract fun people and shame those golf pros and tennis hos.

Moustachio Bashio: Guys grow real "molestaches" and girls sport fake ones.

Ninja Assassins: Tight black clothes, jump kicks, and plastics sword fights.

Homeless Pub Crawl: Bum/crack whore fashion and every crawler has to have a homeless sign (Need money for alcohol research, Ninjas kidnapped my family and I need $4 for karate lessons, or Also available in sober).

Onesie Pub Crawl: Jumpsuits, footy pajamas, Snuggies, wrestling singlets, or spandex bodysuits; try *www.getsnuggie.com* or *www.pajamacity.com*.

Poker Crawl: At every bar, participants get one card. Whoever has the best poker hand at the end of the crawl wins. Green eyeshade visors required.

Zombie Pub Crawl: Stumbling, mindless bodies consuming everything in their path? You don't need much besides torn clothes and good makeup.

Wig Crawl: Start with a Don King and end with a Peg Bundy.

Construction Workers and School Girls: A twist on the priest vs. student costume.

Sugar Mommas and Sugar Daddies Pub Crawl: Guys wear safari outfits and look for rich cougars. Girls wear schoolgirl outfits and gold dig for cradle robbers.

Dead Celebrities: Free drinks for the most recently deceased celebrity costume.

Angry Peasant Mob and Frankenstein: Torches, pitchforks, and angry shouting.

Asians and Godzilla: Crowd running instead of crowd chasing.

Prisoners and Prison Guards: Guys in orange jumpsuits (with fake tattoos). Girls in sexy cop uniforms keeping the chain gang in line.

Hunters and Animals: Have the hunters stalk their prey. Make sure the crawl passes through a public park.

American vs. Roman Gladiators: It's spandex clad 'roid heads vs. sandal-sporting swordsmen.

Bible Pub Crawl: Jesus drank so should you. This is also the only time it's all right to piss your bed sheets.

Protest Pub Crawl: Everyone is responsible for a different protest sign, t-shirt, and chanting slogan. "Nuke a gay baby whale for Jesus!"

Lunch Ladies and Soda Jerks: "How about some more sloppy Joes!"

WRITE YOUR ADDRESS ON YOUR ARM SO THE CABBIE KNOWS WHERE TO DROP YOUR INCOHERENT EXCUSE FOR A LIFELESS BODY.

CHIEF ME! PARTY

The Chief Me Party is a great pre-, actual, or post-party. If you plan on heading out to bars after this party, be ready to sport your penis forehead in public. Meet at a house in jeans and a plain white t-shirt. You are about to get CHIEFED!

Chiefing: The act of decorating/embarrassing a person who is passed out from drinking; see also *shaming*.

THE SET-UP

Gather your friends together and willingly compete in drinking games for the right to "chief" each other. As the host, you'll need to supply Sharpies, duct tape, flour, scissors, note cards, board games, a dictionary, cameras, and copious amounts of alcohol.

The Rules

1. Teams or one-on-one competitors challenge each other to drinking games/competitions.
2. Before each game, one person draws a note card that has a "chiefing punishment" (see our suggested list).
3. The winning team/player gets to pick one person to give the punishment.
4. They can opt out of the punishment up to three times by taking a shot, a really big shot.

Separate people into equally skilled drinking teams of four. The braver partygoers can also challenge each other to one-on-one grudge matches.

Team Challenges

You want to choose group games that move quickly. Try Flip Cup, Boat Race, Anchorman, Suck and Blow, Highest Roll of the Dice, Tallest Human Pyramid (only do once), and Who Can Pop Balloons Faster in Three Different Sexual Positions.

Categories: Both teams stand in a circle. One person picks a category (for example, items in a bag lunch, '80s movies, cartoon characters) and the teammate who stops first, loses.

One-on-One Grudge Matches

As the party gets rocking, weaker links won't be able to keep up with the alcohol intake. In this situation, have teams pick their most talented competitors (drinkers) to represent them in some of these head-to-head games:

- *Handstand Competition (best two out of three)*
- *Beer Bong Race*
- *Freestyle Rap Battle (nonparticipating partygoers select the winner)*
- *Spelling Bee (players open the dictionary to a random page and they each have to pick a word on that page for their opponent to spell)*
- *Ro-Sham-Bo*
- *Bear-Ninja-Cowboy (see Ro-Sham-Bo Tournament)*
- *Thumb Wrestling*
- *Connect Four*
- *The Smiley Game (opponents sit face-to-face and try to make their opponent laugh first without talking)*

The Chiefs

Here are some good suggestions in the table on the facing page to get you started. Good luck Chiefer Sutherlands!

The Chiefs

THE CHIEF	HOW TO PULL IT OFF	5TH YEAR SAYS . . .
The DickFore	Dick on forehead	Simple yet effective when detailed with veins and pubic hair.
The Dr. Evil	Scar drawn over the eye from the forehead to the cheek	Take a picture of them in the pinky-to-mouth Dr. Evil pose.
The Presley	Big sideburns	Bonus points for getting them in an Elvis pose in their tighty whities.
The Hello Kitty	Red nose and black whiskers	You could also make them speak in a Japanese anime accent.
The Harry Potter	Lighting bolt on forehead and glasses around the eyes	Cast disappearing clothes charms. "*Expelliaramus booty shorts!*"
The Rollie Fingers	Curled handlebar mustachio	Bonus points for including the A's logo on their forehead.
The Douche Trifecta	A Superman, barbwire, and Chinese character tattoo	If you want to take it there, include the Ed Hardy logo on their chest.
The Conquistador	Pencil-thin mustache and triangle goatee	Find a pair of gloves to slap people in the face. Then challenge them to a duel (beer chug).
The One Eyed Willie	Pirate eye patch and skull and bones tattoo	And then make them do the Truffle Shuffle.
The Pretty, Pretty Princess	Magic marker nail polish (for guys)	That will make for a great trip to the drugstore the next morning to buy remover.
The Muhammad Ali	Duct-taped hands into fists	Float like a butterfly, drink like a fish.
The Paul Stanley	Black star over right eye and red lips	Do you think Juggalos would have existed without Kiss?
Why So Serious?	The Joker mouth scars from *The Dark Knight*	Just don't do any magic tricks with pencils . . .
The Dicken Pox	Tiny penises all over the face	There is no such thing as too many Sharpie dicks.
The Ninja Turtle	Green face with red or blue eye mask	Or go with red if the person is a hothead shit-talker or orange if he's a mellow stoner type.

OVER THE TOP

If a single Chief isn't enough, you can go all out and really mark up your friends with some full-body art.

For Guys:

Bowtie

Full tuxedo jacket

G-string on his ass crack

Six-pack of canned beer on abs

For Girls:

Baby with an umbilical cord on her stomach

Write "insert here" on her lower back

List her ex-boyfriends in cursive on her arm

Serious bling around her neck and wrists

WAY OVER THE TOP

Everyone's done it, some ridiculous blacked-out act that ruins the night for the rest of your friends—puking on the bar (Darren); shitting liquid raisins on a girl's white couch (Mark); kicking in a plate-glass window to fight a fraternity (Kevin). All your friends can think about is revenge as they drag your comatose ass home. Here are five next-level chiefs that take it *way* over the top and are probably too elaborate to pull off . . . but it'd be fucking hilarious if you did.

1. The Spiderman: Cut fishing wire into strands. Tie one end to a moveable object in his room and the other to his wrist. Do this to as many things you can. When he finally comes to and starts moving, he'll take his whole room with him.

2. The Fake and Bake: Cover your victim in circular label stickers and leave him in the morning sun to roast. He'll wake up with a nice spotted Guido-cheetah finish.

3. The Naked Mile: Get a cardboard box (big enough for a refrigerator, or your passed-out friend). Take off his clothes, stick him in it, and leave him overnight in a public park. When he wakes up he has two options: Get creative with the cardboard box or run the naked mile. Watch from a distance with a couple eighteen packs and binoculars.

4. The Resurrection: Contact the rest of your victim's friends and possibly his family. Have them meet at a funeral home wearing all black. Dress your friend in a suit and place him in front of everyone in a casket. Wait until he wakes up from his blackout. Imagine what would be going through your head if you woke up and popped your head out of a casket and saw your family and friends crying. Amazing.

5. The Mass Murderer: Contact your friendly local police and kindly ask them if they will help you give your friend the best drinking intervention ever. Rip your victim's clothes then cover him in dirt and fake blood. Have the police drop him in the drunk-tank. When he wakes up, have the police come by the cell, stare at him, and say, "You piece of shit." Leave him crying for a few hours or until he attempts suicide . . . then release him and buy him Carl's Jr.

CITIZENSHIP PARTY

The 5th Year has a good friend from Argentina who recently became a U.S. citizen. So obviously, we threw him a party to instruct him on the finer parts of being an American. Making Americans more American . . . just giving back to the community.

THE SET-UP

Not everyone has a friend becoming a U.S. citizen. Remember, this is America; there are plenty of foreigners. Find an exchange student or ethnic coworker that will play along with the theme. Most exchange students are eager for any attention. One party like this can turn them into a goddamn campus celebrity.

Go to Party America and cover the house in über American decor. Buy temporary tattoos to get your guests inked up as they arrive. Red, white, and blue attire is strictly enforced. The guest of honor should sport an American flag like a cape. Just imagine dozens of decked out Americans screaming Springsteen's lyrics, "Born in the USA!" Also, remember to follow each sing along with a deafening "U.S.A." chant. Let freedom ring!

AS PEOPLE FILTER INTO THE PARTY, PUT MATCHING TEMPORARY TATTOOS ON RANDOM GUYS AND GIRLS. TELL THEM TO TRY AND FIND THEIR DRINKING GAME PARTNERS INSIDE. THIS CREATES LITTLE COMPETITIVE TRIBES WITH THE SAME TATTOOS, "EAGLE CLAN UNITE! WE MUST DESTROY THE FLAG CLAN IN FLIP CUP!"

PLAYLIST

Warning! You will wake up without a voice.

"Old Time Rock and Roll"
Bob Seger

"Born in the U.S.A."
Bruce Springsteen

"Louie Louie"
The Kingsmen

"Thunderstruck"
AC/DC

"Why Can't We Be Friends?"
War

"Heat of the Moment"
Asia

"Welcome to the Jungle"
Guns N' Roses

"Rapper's Delight"
The Sugarhill Gang

"Wild Thing"
The Troggs

"Johnny B. Goode"
Chuck Berry

"(I Can't Get No) Satisfaction"
The Rolling Stones

"Hot for Teacher"
Van Halen

"Taking Care of Business"
Bachman-Turner Overdrive

"Here I Go Again"
Whitesnake

"Stay With Me"
Faces

"Stuck in the Middle With You"
Stealers Wheel

"Saturday Night"
Bay City Rollers

"California Girls"
The Beach Boys

"Why Don't We Get Drunk (and Screw)"
Jimmy Buffett

"American Pie"
Don McLean

"Take Me Home, Country Roads"
John Denver

"Small Town"
John Cougar Mellencamp

"Margaritaville"
Jimmy Buffett

"Glory Days"
Bruce Springsteen

"The Joker"
Steve Miller Band

STAY ENTERTAINED

Make the guest of honor perform Tom Cruise's *Risky Business* dance. Clear a space in the living room, give him some Ray Bans and tighty whities then crank Bob Seger's "Old Time Rock and Roll." At the pinnacle of the night, have the guest of honor do the "Pledge of Allegiance." Then do a baptism-style keg stand (four people lift up the honoree and he faces the sky instead of the ground). After his baptism, shower him with beer and then get in a circle to sing "God Bless America."

COLOMBIAN DRUG LORD PARTY

First you get the fake mustache, then you get the girl in the sequin dress, then you slam your head into a mountain of *Scarface* blow (powdered sugar), and smile for the camera. The world is yours! Lock down the compound, round up la familia—it's time to take it to the limit. The CDLP takes the danger out of running a drug cartel, while allowing you to indulge in the drug-educed passion, silky dresses, and ice-cold rum.

THE SET-UP

If you don't have a drug lord's mansion riddled with Uzi bullets, a regular house will do just fine. Gather the houseplants in the main party area. Drug kingpins love foliage. If you can arrange palms, all the better . . . details are everything.

What to Wear When You Kill People for a Living

Men should come dressed in tropical-themed clothes: pastel-colored linen suits, white shoes, Hawaiian or silk shirts, straw Fedora hats, mandatory mustaches (perfect for white powder residue).

Women should come as Latina party girls and trophy wives: Brightly colored evening gowns, fake red nails, lots of glitter, dark eye makeup, sequin tops, excessive amount of faux jewelry, a police wire (wives always lead the cops to the cartel).

What's My Role in the Cartel?

Use poster board to create a cartel family tree. You'll need to pick a family name like Escondito or Vasquez (they scream gold chains and pure white kilos). Then give every partygoer a role within your cartel.

Some possible roles include:

- *The Godfather or El Padron*
- *The Vietnam Vet Turned Drug Smuggling Pilot*
- *Call Girl*
- *Colombian Soap Opera Star*
- *Irish Hitmen*
- *Midlevel Dealers*
- *The Snitch*
- *Undercover DEA Agents*
- *Corrupt Military Generals*
- *Gay Cousin Miami Club Owners*
- *Corrupt Family Accountants*
- *Famous Coke Whores*

Where the Hell Are We?

Here are some tips on how to create the perfect setting for your Villa de Goteo Nasal (nasal drip):

- *Place plants everywhere and buy a sunset photo backdrop.*
- *Put trays of powder out on the table—use powdered sugar, not baking soda.*
- *Rent dick flicks like Scarface and Blow and keep these movies playing throughout the night.*

- *Turn the heat on in the house and run the hot water to give the party a tropical feel.*
- *Keep the drink choices Latino luxurious: mojitos, margaritas, and champagne cocktails (with André of course)*

Dick Flick: The opposite of a chick flick, usually involving zombies or machine guns.

THIS PARTY WILL TURN INTO AN ALL-NIGHT SWEAT-SOAKED DANCE OFF. BLAST THE OBNOXIOUS LATINO MERENGUE AND MAKE YOUR NEIGHBORS FEEL LIKE THEY'RE ON VACATION IN BOGOTA.

PLAYLIST

"Arranca"
Manzanita (*theme song for party*)

"Tu Sonrisa"
Elvis Crespo

"Suavemente"
Elvis Crespo

"Baila Como Es"
Tito Puente

"All for U"
RJD2

"Since '76"
RJD2

"Cha-Cha Rene"
Johnny Pacheco (*limbo song*)

"Mas Que Nada"
Sergio Mendes & Brazil '66

"Baile Latino"
Havana Lounge Music

"Cup of Life"
Ricky Martin

CONGRATULATIONS TO THE CLASS OF 3000

Space . . . the year is 3000. The graduating class from Nebulon 7 has invited you to come enjoy some space juice and music from the fabulous Marglon and the Dinglonites. One last party before the sun hits the earth! The future is now.

The idea of having a future party was inspired by one of the many hungover Sundays that included dark sheets over the windows and sci-fi movie marathons. If you want to relive your high school prom, check out Prom in Your Prime. But if you want to see what the hell high schoolers are going to wear in the future when you're dead and gone—throw this amazing, futuristic event for the ages.

OVER THE TOP

A house party will not do this theme justice. You should really look to rent an event space or gymnasium.

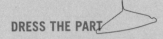

DRESS THE PART

The best thing about this event is trying to predict the future with your costume. Will you go for a space utopian Star Trek uniform or an apocalyptic cyber punk look? The possibilities are endless. Try to make a homemade costume, but if you need a fallback, pick a futuristic movie character.

GUYS	GIRLS
Daft Punk	Milla Jovovich from *Fifth Element*
Tron outfits	Sexy cyborgs
Arnold Schwarzenegger from *Running Man*	Princess Leia (in the slave costume)
Baby Chest Guy (Quato) from *Total Recall*	*Rollerball* girl
Doc or Marty McFly from *Back to the Future*	Daryl Hannah from *Blade Runner*
Woody Allen from *Sleeper*	Barbarella
Bacon Head Guy (Lt. Worf) from *Star Trek*	*Star Trek* skirts
Barf and Lonestar from *SpaceBalls*	An alien—using full body paint

THE SET-UP

Put some work into the decorations and it could be the most epic event of all time. Watch *Blade Runner*, *The Fifth Element*, and *2001: A Space Odyssey* for inspiration. Construct a party-planning committee to help. Use the student council method and divvy up tasks/responsibilities.

Here are some ideas on how to get that awkwardness of a high school dance mixed with a futuristic feel:

- *Tinfoil-wrapped rocks covered in fluorescent paint with black lights*
- *Smoke machines and laser lights*
- *Planetary/cosmic themed backdrop with photography lighting (try* www.dreamworldbackdrops.com *for space-themed backdrops—they actually have some that look like futuristic proms)*
- *Dry ice punch and green Jell-O shots*
- *An elevated stage for the DJ and the master of ceremonies*
- *Go to* www.djwiij.com *and learn how to use Wii controls with turntables or hire a Wii DJ in your area.*

Class of 3000 Superlatives

Hold a ceremony at the end of the night to hand out yearbook-style awards—with a futuristic twist.

- *The Amidala Award—Best Dressed Female*
- *President Skroob Award—Most Likely to Be Intergalactic President*
- *The Chewbacca Award—Biggest Party Animal*
- *The R2D2 Award—Class Clown*
- *The Keanu Reeves—Least Valuable Partier (LVP)*

Least Valuable Partier (LVP): This is the guy who does any of the following: shows up to a party with a bunch of dudes who proceed to act like douche bags and drink all of your booze; gets so drunk that he breaks a bunch of stuff and passes out in his own piss; manages to scare every girl at the party because he's so obnoxiously wasted; always takes the joke *way* too far and offends half the room; doesn't bring a single positive thing to the party.

STAY ENTERTAINED

Keep in the next millennium when it comes to party activities:

Laser Tag

Buy a set of cheap laser tag guns and have Wild West quick draws.

Dance Competition

Have contestants do the robot to Daft Punk's "Robot Rock." Have the master of ceremonies rank the competitors by crowd applause.

In the Year 3000

Take the liberty of creating your own fictitious future (à la Conan O'Brien's segments).

Video Game Tournament

Guitar Hero/DJ Hero Competition/Wii Bowling/Super Mario Galaxy

5TH YEAR LOOKS INTO THE FUTURE

Here are some of things we expect to be going on in the year 3000 . . .

1. Steve Jobs (at over 1,000 years old with a robotic brain) will release the iPack—a jetpack/iPod combo that lets obese kids go *flyking* (hiking while flying).
2. Pfizer will make kabillions marketing their new hybrid drug: Vextasy (one part Viagra, one part ecstasy).
3. The hit reality show will be called *Citizen Games*. Contestants form third world countries will compete against American gladiators for green cards.
4. Everyone will speak Spanish because aliens will have dropped an electromagnetic bomb that destroyed all communication towers except for those of Mexican AM radio channels.
5. When you urinate in toilets, there will be a computer voice that blurts out the STDs you have and the size of your penis.

PLAYLIST

"Tron Legacy Theme"
Daft Punk

"In the Club (On the Street) "
Fanny Games

"Electro Sixteen"
Benny Bennassi ft. Iggy Pop

"Baby"
Pnau (Breakbot remix)

"Punk Thriller"
Loo and Placido

"Cooler Couleur"
Crookers ft. Yelle (Junkie XL remix)

"Hands of God"
Cryptonites

"A Fifth of Beethoven"
Walter Murphy and the Big Apple Band (Soulwax remix)

"The Bottom"
Fukkk Offf (original mix)

"Oh!"
Boys Noize (A-Trak remix)

"Eat It"
Boys Noize

"The Way It Is"
Prodigy

"Circuit"
David Rubato

"Violet Hill"
Coldplay (Cryptonites remix)

"Dodfucksupanescorttune"
Drums of Death

"Never Miss a Beat"
Kaiser Chiefs (Cut Copy remix)

"Stuck on Repeat"
Little Boots (Fake Blood remix)

"Fist of God"
MSTRKRFT

"Am I Wrong"
Etienne de Crecy

"Phantom Part II"
Justice (Boys Noize remix)

COUGAR HUNT: THE BACHELOR PARTY

A typical bachelor party might go something like this: "Hey Broskis, let's get our matching striped shirts pressed, put on our jeans with button back pockets, goop the shit out of our hair, and go to a totally overpriced straddle academy for the worst case of blue balls ever . . . Then we can all brag to each other about how we guarantee our stripper is going to call us when she gets off her shift." How many times have we seen this scenario play out? Don't become the ATM machine for the Vegas bachelor party gauntlet. Plan something different.

THE SET-UP

The Cougar Hunt is a great way to guarantee a night of hilarious pictures while meeting fun older ladies.

Step 1: Go to your local military supply store and buy safari hats (pith helmets) for every guy attending. Buy khaki shirts, safari vests, and khaki shorts. Give an

COUGAR CLASSIFICATIONS

Cougaris Van Halenus:
'80s hair cougar

Cougaris Lexus:
Classy, professional cougar

Cougaris Alpha Felinae:
Overaggressive cougar

Cougaris Divorcis:
Recently divorced on-the-prowl cougar

Cougaris Pupis:
Cougar in training
(age thirty to thirty-four)

award to the guy who wears the shortest pair. Just make sure there is no bubblegum showing.

Step 2: Go to a local toy store and find cheap binoculars to wear around your neck. Also buy a few magnifying glasses for close exams of Caesarean section scars.

Step 3: Wear hiking shoes, loafers, and calf-high brown socks.

Step 4: Go to a costume store for monocles and mustaches. Details count.

Step 5: Print out a Google map route of local "cougar dens" and give it to every safari member just in case one of you becomes cougar bait on the dance floor and gets held up.

Step 6: Go hunt some cougars! Gather as much evidence as possible . . . scientific documentation, or photographs.

Step 7: Bring "Hello My Name Is" stickers to tag and photograph different classifications of cougars.

Eight Cougar-Hunting Tips

1. Cougars love happy hour and can be found at local watering holes around dusk. For maximum CBP (cougar bagging potential), think about getting an early start on the night.
2. Remember, cougars are in their sexual prime and prefer to hunt rather than be hunted. They enjoy the role reversal, so play it cool and don't make any sudden movements or proposals. Before you know it, you'll be in her Audi headed back to her new condo.
3. Send in a cougar scout to every bar. This hunter should use his binoculars to scan the room and see if the grounds are worth hunting. Then just imagine as bar patrons watch him wave in his fellow cougar connoisseurs.
4. Beware of '80s music. Cougars were in their prime in the '80s and will pull you into their cougar den (i.e., dance floor).
5. Cougars feel very safe in hotel bars. Use these as a failsafe last resort.
6. If all else fails, start taking about how you started a nonprofit charity for abused Boston Terriers. Cougars love nonprofit charities and little dogs.
7. Don't make the fatal mistake of buying beer for a cougar. Martinis are the cougar's drink of choice.
8. Assign names to the cougar-hunting party. No one hunts better than aristocratic English gentlemen. Make sure your group all have "Hello My Name Is" stickers with some of these names:
   Sir Edmund Cockington
   Sir Duncan Fluffington
   Arch Duke Richard Sexington III
   Ethan Muffinton IV
   Charles Twatington II
   Sir Edward Cornholer
   Prince Phillip Buggerton
   Humphrey Potscotton
   Theodore Toppletime Esquire

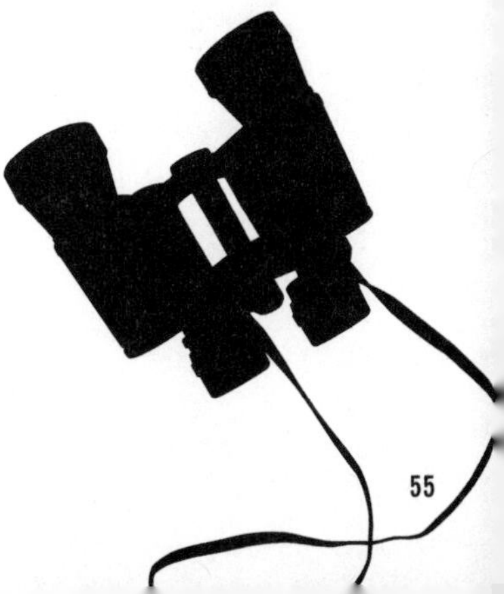

CROQUET PAR-TAY

"I would like to make a toast . . . Here's to pastel polo shirts, argyle sweaters, prescription drugs, and not wearing socks with your boat shoes."

The East Coast contingent of WASP-y socialites have given us yet another practice to ridicule . . . croquet! All right you, Princes of New England and Goddesses of The Cape, get your summer's best out of the trunk and prepare for a day of plaid pants and high fives. You and your trust funds are cordially invited to the Collins Family Croquet Invitational.

THE SET-UP

The Croquet Par-tay requires a large lawn space and a few croquet sets. (You can find a cheap set for around $30 to $50 at a sporting goods store.) Croquet is played by six people at a time and coincidentally there are six members of the Collins family. Put all of the family members' names in a hat and pull randomly to determine your ball color.

The point of croquet is to hit your colored ball through all six wickets first. The balls must go through the front of the wicket and cannot go through backwards. If your ball goes through a wicket, you get an additional bonus stroke. If your ball hits another player's ball you have three options:

1. You can play as they lie and use a bonus stroke to keep advancing to the next wicket.
2. You can place your ball directly next to your opponent's ball, use your foot to hold your own ball, and then blast your opponent's ball in the opposite direction.
3. You can move your opponent's ball one mallet head away from your own ball and use your bonus stroke to continue playing.

The first Collins family member to get through the last wicket wins Grandpa Collins' inheritance! Remember, making business deals is also a common activity on the croquet field . . . "I'll sell my daughter's virginity for the logging rights in the Amazonian rainforest; what do you say?" "Deal!"

MEET THE COLLINS FAMILY

The color of your ball is important because it decides the order of players as well as your drink for the tournament.

1st ...... Blue: Tom Collins

2nd ..... Red: Brandy Collins

3rd ...... Black: Jon Collins

4th ...... Yellow: Mike Collins

5th ...... Green: Vivian Collins

6th ...... Orange: Pedro Collins

For those of you not familiar with the Collins family, let me introduce them:

Tom Collins, the patriarch:
Gin, lemon juice, club soda, and sugar

Brandy Collins, his gold-digging wife:
Brandy, lemon juice, club soda, and sugar

Jon Collins, the alcoholic, womanizing son:
Bourbon, lemon juice, club soda, and sugar

Mike Collins, the Harvard dropout:
Whiskey, lemon juice, club soda, and sugar

Vivian Collins, the slutty socialite:
Vodka, lemon juice, club soda, and sugar

Pedro Collins, the illegitimate son:
Rum, lemon juice, club soda, and sugar

DAY AT THE TRACK

Welcome to another beautiful day at the horse track. Cigar smoke is wafting through the air, the beer is flowing like wine, and the combination of hope plus desperation is feeding those jockeys dinner tonight . . . and they're off.

THE SET-UP

Organize a midsized group of friends who don't mind laying down some cash on a few ponies. Rent a yellow school bus for group transportation, and drink heavily on your way to the track.

A day in the sun, betting on the ponies, sipping back on a few cold ones, along with a drunken bus ride home cannot be topped. Whenever you are looking for something new to do with your friends, consider a day at the track. This event is easy enough to plan . . . just find that yellow school bus.

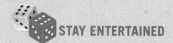

STAY ENTERTAINED

Typically, a track will hold ten races a day. Before the races start, write down the different horses' numbers and have everyone pick one out of a hat. That's their horse. (If there are more partiers than horses, put the numbers back in the hat so that multiple people will be assigned the same horse.)

1st Race: Mint Julep Round—No day at the track is complete without the go-to drink of the Kentucky Derby. If your pony wins (comes in first), places (comes in second), or shows (comes in third), then everyone else has to buy you and the other top finishers mint juleps.

Note: Can substitute with a cranberry bourbon punch if preferred.

2nd Race: Nachos Round—Every horse track in America sells 7-Eleven-style, gremlin cheese nachos littered with delicious jalapeños. The people with the last three horses have to buy nachos for the group. It's important to get an ozone-like base of chemical cheese coating your stomach before the Jack Daniels shots start burning it like UV rays.

3rd Race: Birthday Round—This is a team round, so forget your individual horses. Those partiers born between January and June pick one horse and those born between July and December pick another. The group whose horse finishes lower in the rank has to buy beers for the winners.

4th Race: Ask a Stranger Round—Everyone has to go up to a random person and ask them what they're betting on this race. Then they place the same bet on their horse. Buy your new friend a beer if your horse brings home the bacon.

5th Race: Girls vs. Guys Round—Another team round: Have a male and female delegate pick a horse number out of the hat. The gender with the losing horse has to go to the bathroom together, squeeze into one stall, and take a funny picture. Immediately, show it to the opposite sex and then upload to Facebook.

6th Race: Trifecta Box Round—A trifecta is when you pick three horses to finish in the top three in any order. You can make $6 or $12 bets. These are fun because the payoffs are higher.

7th Race: Best Horse Name—Forget the assigned horse and go with whichever one has the best name. Whoever picks the winning horse has to go and get their picture taken with it.

8th Race: Best Jockey Name—Same as above—except instead of picking based on the name of a half-ton beast, it's up to a ninety-pound shrimp.

9th Race: Last in Show—Have everyone put in three or five bucks so you can run your own betting operation. Whoever has the last place horse wins the pot (or splits it if more than one person is assigned to the horse).

10th Race: Group Bet—It's good to end betting on the same horse. Discuss and pick a pony to win it all. Up the ante and have everyone throw in $10. If the horse wins, use the money to tip the bus driver and buy champagne for the ride home.

DRESS THE PART

The contrast in costumes will make for some kickass pictures.

Costumes for men scream "winner, winner, chicken dinner!":

Tight plaid pants

Polyester shirts

Gold chains

Sunglasses

Mustaches

Newsy hats

White loafers

Brut Cologne

Women tend to gravitate more towards the spectator gold digger look:

Sundresses

Sun hats

Large glasses

High heels

Sweaters tied round the neck

Pearls

Obnoxiously huge diamond rings

An always-present of Chardonnay

NAME YOUR PONY

Once our line of caffeinated nacho cheese, called Nacho Average Cheese, makes us billions of dollars, 5th Year will naturally have to buy a racehorse to show off our exorbitant excess of money. Here are some of the names we're considering:

- Lady Gaga's Dangling Labias
- Goblincock
- Clit Eastwood
- Queen Elizabeth's Erection
- Yeastiality
- Smegma-saurus Rex
- Queefing Beauty
- Thundercock Jenkins
- Cock Cheese O'Callaghan
- Duchess Cunt Fungus

Note: These also make great nicknames for your friends.

DONKEY PUNCH DINNER PARTY

A classy dinner party has its place in the world, but certainly not in this book. Being polite at the dinner table is boring and lame—everyone knows that. What if there was a dinner party that features the most offensive and disgustingly named dishes that you can imagine? Genius! The Donkey Punch Dinner Party is not good for Aunt Sharon's Bible study group, but it is great if you are a sick, twisted individual who likes to laugh about eating a Hot Carl Sloppy Joe while dipping it into some Dirty Sanchez Seven-Layer Dip. Get nasty, and plan a feast that can entertain a crowd on multiple levels.

THE SET-UP

Go to the web to find some sick, sexually perverted names (or check out the list on the next page). We're not saying you should actually *put* diarrhea in your sloppy Joe mix—who do you think we are, sickos? We're just saying it's more fun if you name your meatball subs the Cleveland Steamers.

Everyone attending is responsible for bringing their own sexually explicit dinner or dessert dish that is appropriately labeled. Coming up with a name for your dish is the fun part, and seeing what your guests bring will guarantee some laughs.

As the host, you're responsible for brewing up a big batch of Donkey Punch. There are a million different punch recipes online but most use three bottles of cranberry juice, two liters of ginger ale, and one bottle of Captain Morgan's, with some floating pineapple chunks for effect.

SLAP GOLDEN SHOWER ALE LABELS ON ALL THE BEER THAT'S BEING CONSUMED.

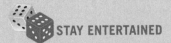

STAY ENTERTAINED

You should also print out a big list of perverted sexual terms and other slang from websites like *www.UrbanDictionary.com*. After your Blumpkin Pumpkin Pie and a few glasses of Donkey Punch, play some perverted Pictionary in the living room.

Food Ideas*

Blumpkin Pumpkin Pie

Angry Dragon Sushi Rolls

Arabian Goggle Kabobs

Cleveland Steamer Meatballs

Rusty Trombone Tiramisu

Dutch Oven Biscuits

Hot Carl Sloppy Joes

Alabama Hot Pockets

Mississippi Mudflap Brownies

Blue Balls Muffins

Cincinnati Bowtie Pasta

Tossed Fruit Salad with Pearl Necklace Glaze

Dirty Sanchez Seven-Layer Dip

Felcher Cannolis

*All definitions can be found on *www.urbandictionary.com*; call Mom to get the actual recipes—she'll be so proud.

SICK CHARADES

If you'd prefer to use your acting abilities as opposed to your drawing ones, you can the equally twisted Sick Charades. The point of charades is not to win by picking difficult topics like *On Golden Pond*; the point is to try and embarrass the other team as much as possible.

Note: If you don't know how to play charades, don't waste our time. Check out the rules on Wikipedia.

Categories:

Films: Indicated by pretending to crank an old fashioned film camera

TV: Indicated by making a square box in front with your index fingers

Person: Indicated by standing with your hands on hips

Location: Indicated by making a circle in your hand and pointing to it

Perverted: Indicated by humping motion

Funny Examples:

Films: *Deliverance*; *What's Eating Gilbert Grape*; *Pulp Fiction*; *Brokeback Mountain*; *Showgirls*; *You Got Served*; *Stomp the Yard*; *Drop Dead Fred*; *Misery*; *The Day After Tomorrow*; *Godzilla*; *The Little Mermaid; Teen Wolf*; *Weekend at Bernie's*

TV: *Moesha*; *David the Gnome*; *Alf*; *Out of this World*; *Quantum Leap*; *Are You Afraid of the Dark?*; *Teddy Ruxpin*; *MacGyver*; *American Gladiators*; *Mighty Morphin Power Rangers*; *Hey Dude*

Person: Monica Lewinsky; James Woods; Chuck Norris; Danny Devito; Freddy Mercury; Will Smith; Jean Claude Van Damme; Tara Reid; Kevin Federline; Elmer Fudd; Chewbacca; Richard Gere (with his gerbil); Mike Tyson; Mel Gibson; Anna Nicole Smith; Steve-o; R. Kelly; Lorena Bobbit

Location: STD clinic; Raiders game; India; Mexico; Orange County; Leper Colony; Detroit; Cancun; Canada; sex shop

Perverted: Fetus; STDs; snowball; teabag; upper-deck; blumpie; rimjob; golden shower; pearl necklace; explosive diarrhea; necrophiliac; premature ejaculation; blue balls; nymphomaniac; bestiality

DOUCHE VS. HIPSTER PARTY

Douche: "I wear way too much AXE; I spike my hair with Dep cause it's hard. I sport jeans that have button fly back pockets and rips all over cause it's dope. I wear either overdesigned, bedazzled über tight t-shirts or striped pink and green button-up shirts 'cause everyone else does. I wear sunglasses indoors at night because it makes me better looking. I'm basically really fucking sweet."

Hipster: "The last time I washed my hair was, whatever bro . . . you wouldn't understand; I'm fucking ironic . . . just look at my fluorescent orange shooting vest I'm wearing . . . and did I show you my numb-chucks? Pretty fucking original and ironic, huh? Dude, whatever, you wouldn't understand because you're a racist, bro . . . it's all about indie rock, PBR, tight black pants, dancing shoes, complaining about stuff, and whining. Whatever, bro."

So are you more of a Douche or a Hipster?
Admit it, 'cause you know you're one or the other.

THE SET-UP

There's a civil war of youth raging and kids across America are picking colors like it's Compton in the '90s. These two factions consolidated subcultures so quickly that nightlife has become a purely bipartisan system. It's time for you to host a battle between the douches and the hipsters. May the best over-accessorized subculture win.

CHOOSE SIDES

Do you wear bedazzled tiger shirts or overly ironic t-shirts? Pick your side and the costume will follow.

Hipsters swallowed the Indie Rockers, Fashionistas, Emos, Skaters, Asians, Trust Fund Artists, Electronic DJs, Glam Rockers, Heroin Chic Male/Female Model, Graffiti Artists, Underground Hip-Hop, and Green Vegan Credit Card Hippies.

The Douchey's swallowed the MMA Affliction Douches, Persians, Lake Trash Meatheads, The Guidos, Prep School Abercrombie Kids, Club Promoters, Sorority Girls, Fraternity Guys, Body Builders, New Jersey, Orange County, and San Diego.

STAY ENTERTAINED

Focus on group-drinking games.

Anchorman
Page 21

Beer Pong Tournaments
Page 21

Speed Quarters
Page 21

Beer Darts
Page 22

Survivor Flip Cup
Page 22

DRESS AS YOU DID AS A KID

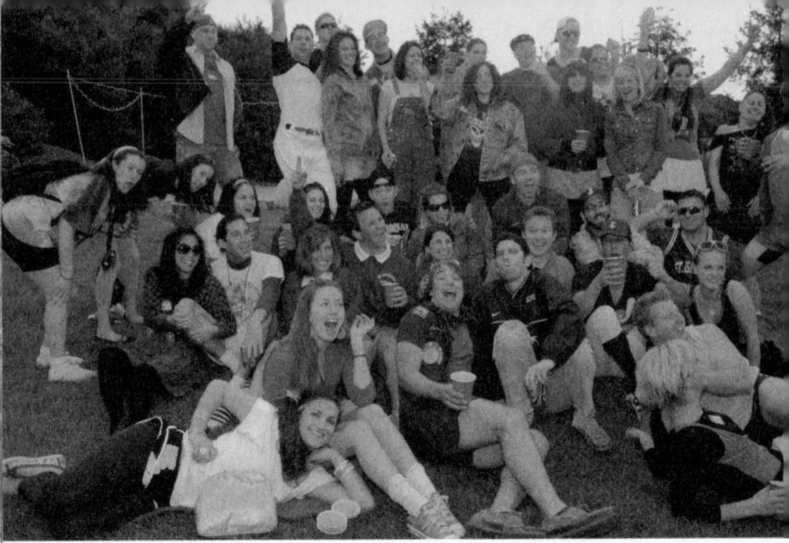

I was ten years old and walking home from a Little League game when I couldn't hold it anymore. I crapped my pants. I was wearing kelly green Cheeta sweat pants, Reebok pumps, and a bright purple turtleneck. All of it was in style back then . . . except for the poop in my pants.

Hyper-color. Slap bracelets. Spin the bottle. Stuffed bras, retainers, and Cross Colors overalls. Despite how old you are, you probably wore some pretty sweet digs when you were ten years old. These are the clothes of your generation. Embrace your roots. Being born in 1975 or 1985 it doesn't matter, find an ugly, hideous, and embarrassing picture of yourself from childhood, and match that outfit. This is the Dress as You Did as a Kid party.

THE SET-UP

Get your parents involved. Have them find a hilarious picture you can recreate. Focus on the third- to sixth-grade "danger zone" for awesome prepubescent outfits.

Every partygoer is responsible for bringing a birthday present from your preteen era. Toys could include:

- *Pogs*
- *Slap bracelets*
- *Muscle Men*
- *Garbage Pail Kids*
- *Super Soakers*
- *Madballs*
- *Nerf guns*
- *Reebok Pumps*

GO TO WWW.EBAY.COM OR WWW.RETROJUNK.COM FOR MORE IDEAS AND PLACES TO BUY THESE KICKASS THROWBACK TOYS. GETTING PRESENTS FOR YOUR BIRTHDAY WAS SO COOL.

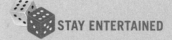

STAY ENTERTAINED

Here are a few games that'll take partygoers down memory lane.

TV Sitcom Theme Song Showdown

Download about thirty theme songs from TV shows and make a CD. Whoever guesses the correct TV show gets to pick someone to do a Franzia chug (Franzia is mandatory for most parties). Here's a good website with free downloads: *www.slackerup.com/TVThemes.*

Chubby Bunny

This one's for the girls. Every contestant starts with two marshmallows in her mouth. Each has to clearly say the words, "chubby bunny" to advance to the next round. If she advances, give her another marshmallow to put in her mouth. Play until there is one clear winner.

Truth, Dare, or Trivia

Give every partygoer a flashcard number. Girls are odds; guys are even. Pull out random numbers and the girl/guy combo gets a truth challenge, dare challenge, or trivia challenge. For successful trivia answers, the combo could allocate a Jell-O shot to any person.

continued

Throwback Trivia

Name three characters from *The Land Before Time.*
Answers: Ducky, Cera, Spike, Littlefoot, and Petrie

What was the name of the mountain in the TV show *Guts*?
Answer: Aggro Crag

What is the name of the principal in *Beavis and Butthead*?
Answer: Principal McVicker

In the movie *Sandlot*, who makes out with Wendy Peffercorn?
Answer: Michael "Squints" Paladores

In the show *Out of This World*, what was Eve Ethel Garland's special power and how did she do it?
Answer: She could freeze time by putting her two fingers together.

What was the name of Pete's tattoo in the show *Adventures of Pete and Pete.*
Answer: Petunia

In the show *Clarissa Explains It All*, what was the name of her annoying bratty brother?
Answer: Ferguson Darling

What were the names of the three nephews on *DuckTales*?
Answer: Huey, Duey, and Luey

In the TV show *Dinosaurs*, what was the baby's favorite line?
Answer: "Not the Mama."

In 1991 Nickelodeon launched three new animated series. Name two.
Answer: *Doug, Rugrats, or Ren and Stimpy*

What was the name of the TV show where contestants competed in live action video games like Ghouls and Ghosts?
Answer: *Nickelodeon Arcade*

Name the board game where a computer would give you a sequence of different colored light flashes and you would have to repeat them in order.
Answer: Simon

On the show *Full House* what was the name of DJ Tanner's best friend?
Answer: Kimmy Gibler

Name two characters from the show *Hey Dude.*
Answer: Lucy, Melody, Danny, Mr. Ernst, Buddy, Brad, Ted, and Jake

Name the other five main characters (first and last names) from *Saved by the Bell* besides Zach Morris.
Answer: Lisa Turtle, AC Slater, Screech Powers, Jesse Spano, Kelly Kapowski, and Richard Belding

DRUNK DEBATES

Nearly everything can be debated. This is why we mix booze, debates, and mildly intelligent people and end up with live entertainment. In fact, statistics show the average person's debate skills improve 38.6 percent when intoxicated.*

THE SET-UP

This activity should be played with a smaller group of friends, and is best with no more than twenty-five people.

1. Pick two of your friends who are verbally aggressive and can bullshit their way out of any situation.
2. Get everyone at the party to write two debate topics each.
3. Collect them and mix them up in a hat.
4. The master of ceremonies is in charge of picking the topics out of the hat. He/she will decide whether the topic is worthy of a debate.

*Again, this "fact" came right out of our ass.

5. Announce the chosen topic to the party. Flip a coin to have the debaters choose their side of the topic.

The Drunk Debate Structure

Note: all structure is usually thrown out the window when people get drunk—and it's funnier that way:

A: *Opening Positive Remarks:* 60 seconds
B: *Negative Rebuttal:* 60 seconds
A: *Second Positive Remarks:* 60 seconds
B: *Cross Examination:* 30 seconds

Always remember your SPEERM topics while formulating your debate:

S = Social
P = Political
E = Economic
E = Environmental
R = Religious
M = Moral

After remarks have been made, the crowd will get the chance to vote for the winner. This is done in one of two ways: secret ballot or drunken cheers. Winners are not necessarily chosen because of the validity of their arguments . . . sometimes the people who are funny as hell and make no logical sense win on entertainment points. Be outrageous and you will win the crowd.

Twenty Drunk Debate Topics

- *Pet monkey* vs. *pet tiger* (which one would be cooler)
- *Full pubes* vs. *shaved pubes*
- *Burritos* vs. *burgers*
- *Chris Farley* vs. *John Belushi*
- *Day drinking* vs. *night drinking*
- *The ability to fly* vs. *the ability to freeze time*
- *Bacon* vs. *cheese*
- *Reading books* vs. *playing video games*
- *Brad Pitt movies* vs. *Russell Crowe movies*
- *Masturbating* vs. *taking a big dump*
- *Cocaine* vs. *marijuana*
- *Fake boobs* vs. *real boobs*
- *Bob Marley* vs. *Tupac* (who had more impact)
- *Internet porn* vs. *the NFL* (which is more entertaining)
- *Monogamy* vs. *polygamy*
- *Michael Jackson* vs. *Kanye West* (who is the King of Pop)
- *Junior high* vs. *high school* (which was more traumatic)
- *Hangovers or TV commercials* (which would you get rid of)

TAKE IT TO THE 'NET

Don't let the Drunk Debates stop just because the workweek starts. Take them to the World Wide Web. All you need is a bunch of bored friends who prefer to check their Gmail than actually do their work. Here are ten topics to get the e-mail chains going:

1. 2012 Doomsday Scenarios: Will the Gingers be the only race able to thrive without sunlight or will 3,000 rich Americans nuke everyone and move to a tropical island where they are all stars on their own reality shows?

2. The Best Funeral Plans: A Hawaiian luau with your roasted dead body, being sent down an Olympic ski jump in a tuxedo and casket, getting carried into a strip club wearing sunglasses (*Weekend at Bernie's*-style) and left on tip row, or hiring an actor to tell you're family that you were a CIA agent.

3. Where Everyone Knows Your Name: If I had an unlimited budget to open a bar, it would be called . . .

4. Lessons from Feldman: What was the most valuable life lesson learned from and '80s movie? (Include YouTube clips.)

5. The Kanye West Writing Contest: Without stopping, see how long you can talk about how cool you are. As soon as you stop typing for more than ten seconds, the exercise is over and you have to send out your train of thought.

6. Super Mario Who?: If I could design any video game, it would be called . . .

7. Easy as Pie: Break down your friends' personalities by how alike they are to fictional television and movie characters (Ryan's 20 percent Zach Morris, 25 percent MC Gusto, 15 percent Marty McFly, 10 percent Duckie, 20 percent George-Michael Bluth, and 5 percent Michelle Tanner). Make a pie chart for each one.

8. Life of the Party: Rank your friends based on their partying abilities. Use the same kind of scientific system employed by the BCS, giving weight to the number of outings they attend, consistency in getting drunk, and ability to generate great stories compared to their number of losses (arrests, being thrown out of bars, starting fights, or puking).

9. Separated at Birth: Everyone must find Web images that look like everyone else on the e-mail chain.

10. Douche Madness: Create a NCCA-style bracket with the top sixty-four douche bags. Vote on who advances in each round.

DUCT TAPE KUMITE

Fighters from around the world come to wage war in the oldest fighting tournament known to man. Of course, I am talking about the Kumite from the legendary movie *Bloodsport* with JCVD. This version involves duct taping your limbs and fighting like retarded arthritic bears. Bow to your sensei.

THE SET-UP

Step 1: Organize a Bloodsport Kumite Tournament.

Stage this event at a baseball field or some type of soft outdoor surface; or if you have an underground death fighting arena, use that.

Step 2: Immobilize Yourself.

Gather old magazines, used books, or phone books. Buy ten rolls of duct tape. The point of this event is to inhibit the use of one's joints (both arms and legs) by taping them straight. Put the magazine or book on the inside of the arm and have someone tape it down. This step should be repeated on the other arm and on the back of each leg. It is really important that each person is taped down well, because any ability to bend your joints is an illegal advantage. Be sure to securely fasten all books. All players should have the mobility of a stick figure.

Step 3: Fight to the Death! (Not really, but we wish.)

After the joints are taped, have the referee tape up everyone's hands into fists. Grabbing is not an option. You need one person out of the event to tape everyone up and also pour beer into people's mouths, which is close to impossible with your joints immobilized. (Try it . . . it's depressing.)

The Rules

1. Pair everyone off into tag teams and have them come up with a team name that relates to a 1980s action movie.
2. Once the teams are set, have a relay race to set the order of fights: First place vs. fourth and second vs. third. This is hilarious.
3. The point of the Kumite is to try and knock over the other team's players. Each knockdown counts as one point and starts a new round.
4. The first team to get three knockdowns advances to the next round.
5. The two winning teams advance to the championship round of the Kumite.

After the team championship, have an all-out Kumite with every contestant to see who is worthy of fighting Chong Li and his giant moobs in the final match.

Moobs: Man boobs.

ENGLISH OPPRESSION DAY/ ST. PATRICK'S DAY

St. Patrick's Day has been hijacked by amateurs, who use the holiday as an excuse to get plastered. It's insulting. It's like a hooker who can't give hand jobs on Halloween because there's a bunch of sorority girls moonlighting in streetwalker costumes. Irish folk live the other 364 days of the year in a constant fog of guilt-ridden inebriation. (5th Year is 150 percent Irish; the other 50 percent is Eggplant . . . *ahem* . . . I mean Sicilian.)

THE SET-UP

In the true rebellious nature of the Celtic people, flip the switch and insult the original imperial power. Plan your own English Oppression Day. Dress up like stereotypical Englishmen and mock the island of wig-wearing inbreeds.

Costumes choices can include:

- *William Shakespeare*
- *English schoolboys*
- *Barristers*
- *Sherlock Holmes*
- *Harry Potter*
- *Colonial explorers*
- *David Beckham*
- *Soccer hooligans*
- *Hot girls dressed as British royalty*
- *Hot girls dressed in green so people know you are joking*

After you've picked out your costumes, parade yourselves around town—to English pubs, of course. Drink Boddingtons's beer and speak in horrible accents while spitting on the people you're talking to. Dressing up like oppressive Englishmen may create some uneasy feelings with the local crowds, so bring plenty of good-looking girls to alleviate any offended bar dwellers. Tell those old punch-drunk Irishmen that you're ridiculing their hemophiliac oppressive neighbors. Then buy them a shot of Bushmills. It usually works out just fine after that.

*For the modern Englishman look, wear green Billy Bob teeth, white Puma shoes, and a tight polo shirt that exposes your pint belly and twelve-year-old-girl biceps.

STAY ENTERTAINED

Good transportation was the foundation of the British Empire. If you live in a big city, rent a double-decker bus like you'd see on the streets of London. That was the cherry, or should I say *sherry*, on top of our Oppression Day. The open-topped bus allowed us to get as silly drunk as possible, and not worry about crashing our horse-drawn carriages. Be safe: No puking or peeing off of the top, and no English vs. Irish brawls. Dear God, please no.

EURO TRASH BASH

Euro trash (n.): mildly derisive term used by North Americans; refers to Europeans who speak broken English; wear gaudy clothing that is probably fashionable where they come from, but isn't here; use a threatening amount of cologne; and always look like they are about to take Ecstasy and go to a rave.

When you don't like something here in America, you either punch it or make fun of it. You don't want to stain your No Fear shirt fighting a chain-smoking socialist. Instead, celebrate Euro-phobia by throwing the Euro Trash Bash.

THE SET-UP

The first step to planning such a momentous night is picking outfits. Go to a cheap department store with your friends, invade the women's section, and try on anything that is shiny and tight. If your friends start laughing at your New York glitter shirt and capri pants, you're on the right track. Don't forget the finishing touches with some extreme partying glasses (color tinted). After your way too tight outfit has been assembled, it's time to figure out "Who am I and what country am I from?" Are you Sergio from Italy, a fashion photographer who thinks every girl he meets should model? Or Yuri, a DJ from the Germany who ships his Benz to the Autobahn every year and gets rim-jobs from Katinka the heiress to the fur coat industry? "Come on baby. Let's sex just once and see how you feel about my sprocken in your dichenhole."

Throw your names, countries of origin, and occupations on "Hello My Name Is" stickers so all those "super-cool American fun-time party girls" know what's up. If you choose to go out rather than have a house party, agree that if anyone is caught speaking out of character they must buy the whole group a round of drinks. And if you do go out, be sure to pick one of those douche bag hotspots that is overflowing with commercial realtors in striped shirts. At least one-quarter of those fucktards will believe you are actually European.

PLAYLIST

Loud and aggressive but good techno:

"I Love My Sex"
Benassi Bros.

"I Like the Way"
Bodyrockers

"Slam"
Pendulum

"Put Your Hands Up"
Benny Benassi

"Rock My Body"
Felix da Housecat

"Say, Say, Say"
Hi Tack (Radio Mix)

"Do It"
Junior Jack

"Eisaber"
DJ Dan

"Emerge"
Fischerspooner

"Shiny Disco Balls"
Who Da Funk

"Call on Me"
Eric Prydz

"One More Time"
Daft Punk

"Alive"
Daft Punk

"Idealistic"
Digitalism

"Easy Love"
MSTRKRFT

"White Horse"
Wonderland Ave.

"Genesis"
Justice

"D.A.N.C.E."
Justice

"Strict Machine"
Goldfrapp

Scorecard for Euro Trash Night

Here's an aggressively offensive Euro Trash checklist to give the night a competitive twist. Keep track of everyone's points and the winner should get a free breakfast. Last time we played this game, it ended with a homeless man smashing a guitar over Connor's face. No joke. E-mail us and we will send you the video.

One Point

- ❑ Dance on the bar in capri pants.
- ❑ Get the DJ to play "Love Generation" by Bob Sinclair.
- ❑ Be the one to sport the lowest V-neck t-shirt.
- ❑ Have the largest, most visible designer label on your clothes.
- ❑ Try to put a round of drinks on your Gap card.

Two Points

- ❑ Wear a man-purse the entire night.
- ❑ Don't wear deodorant the entire night.
- ❑ YouTube "Tecktonik Dancing" and re-enact it on the dance floor.
- ❑ Use a whole bottle of self-tanner—just on your face.
- ❑ Wear three pastel polo shirts with all of the collars popped.

INTRODUCE YOURSELF TO EVERYBODY IN THE BAR—ESPECIALLY THEIR GIRLFRIENDS. YOU WILL LEARN THAT A BAD ACCENT AND BOLD MOVES WILL INTIMIDATE EVEN THE BIGGEST DOUCHES. "HEY, BABIES. ANYONE VANT TO DISCO DANCE WITH HOTTEST ÜBER SEX MACHINE, DEITER?" IF YOU PISS SOMEONE OFF, YOU CAN PLAY THE "I NO UNDERSTAND ENGLISH" CARD.

Three Points

- ❑ Smoke five cigarettes in five minutes.
- ❑ Shave your hair into one of those fucked-up mullet/fauxhawk haircuts.
- ❑ Use glow sticks on the dance floor.
- ❑ Fart on the dance floor and keep dancing until you're the last one there.
- ❑ Spray a whole bottle of cheap cologne all over yourself before going out.

FIVE ENTERTAINING THINGS TO DO AT A SHITTY PARTY

Part of coming up with a formula for a good party meant that we had to go to a good amount of shitty parties. There's nothing worse than a fuck job of a party. The party becomes something people have to deal with instead of enjoy. When I get bored at a party, and I can't leave right away (for politeness issues), I find new ways to entertain myself. You'll know you're at a shit shindig if you see any of the following when you arrive:

- *It's a garbage-filled, disgusting pig sty.*
- *Everyone but you is really stoned.*
- *Everyone but you is really drunk—and the party just started.*
- *There's a lopsided gender ratio.*
- *There are no basic necessities (cups, toilet paper, etc.).*
- *Everyone is watching TV instead of socializing.*
- *Groups of people are clustered together in different corners of the house and the host thinks it's okay.*
- *Nobody greets you at the door with a beer.*
- *People are stealing shoes and vandalizing the house.*

It's time to manufacture some entertainment. After all, you probably had some thing much better to do, but you decided to spend your precious time at someone's party. To make the most of the party is to make the most out of life. If you're bored, you're boring. Here are five things to do at a shitty party.

1. Start talking to strangers: This can be the best thing you can do at a party. Most people are begging to be talked to . . . they're just scared to make the first move. They have all kinds of weird stuff to tell you I promise. When the noise level starts to get high, it means people are talking and having fun. Good sign. I would recommend doing this first and then when you know a couple randoms, you can get them to play some stupid games with you when you ask. And they'll all eagerly say yes.

2. Accomplish a house mission: Survey the house for games, music, and entertainment. Most people have interesting stuff laying around. They think its boring cause they see it every day, doesn't mean its not cool. Also, you can scour the house for food to cook. People love to eat, and chances are this shitty party has nothing to consume. Grilled cheese, popcorn, or PB and J squares are usually laying around. Cook and deliver.

3. Volunteer for a party job: Most hosts can't do it on their own, so volunteer. Typical jobs are the BBQ guy; keg guy; photographer focused on getting the most insane pictures ever.

4. Mix some kick ass alcoholic concoctions: People love drinking exotic drinks, so Google drink recipes on your phone, gather your ingredients, and fire up the blender. People will be excited and grateful for the frothy goodness.

5. Organize a game: Pick something nobody has ever heard of and get all your new friends to play with you. This can be something you make up, or something that you've playing in some far off drinking land. Starting a small game with a mini-group will be easier to get peoples attention. Most people don't want to do something new and scary, so starting small might help get the ball rolling. During the game, think of the best story you've ever heard, and tell it using loud emphasis on noises. The excitement of your story and the game will wake people up—people will flock to your game like flies to poopy diapers.

A party usually sucks because the host has put in zero effort to make it enjoyable. That's his fault. It doesn't mean the party is totally ruined. Most parties are salvageable. Don't wait for someone else to show you a good time; step up and create a situation that you'll want to retell over eggs the next morning. That's what it's all about.

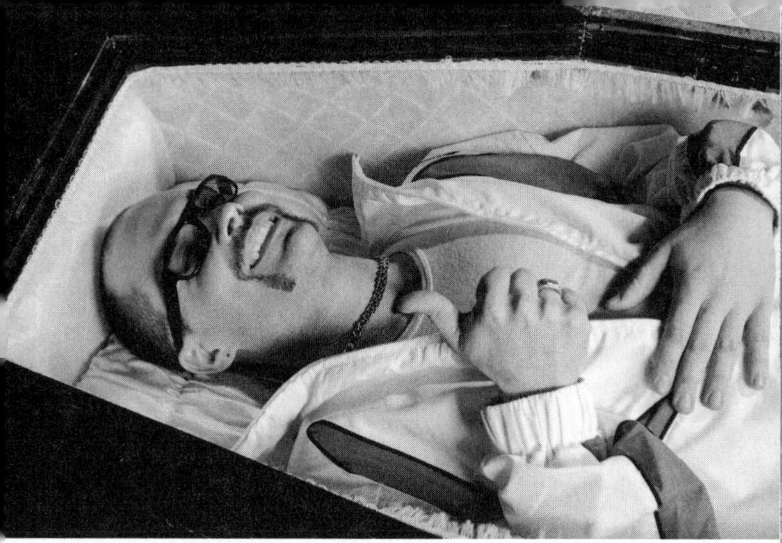

THE FAKE WAKE

Yes, it's a little morbid. Just think of it as a roast where everyone is wearing black. The key to a great Fake Wake is picking the perfect candidate. It can't be Wendy Whitepanties or Dave DiAngelo the All-American Quarterback. This event only works for your friend who is most often described with the phrase, "Did you hear what that (insert: fuckstain, shithead, asshole) did last night?" Pick the person that has the uncanny ability of finding trouble. This person will have plenty of roast-able material. Everyone's got one friend like this, so when their birthday rolls around, think of throwing this party.

THE SET-UP

1. Find a theater, comedy venue, community center, or banquet hall that you can rent. Make sure it's walking distance to a good dive bar. If you can't afford to rent, a backyard will do just fine.

2. Warn them that you're coming in to binge drink with a fake dead person.

3. Build a fake coffin with the help of a Home Depot employee with a sense of humor. Make sure it's sturdy enough to prop up during the roast.

4. Send out an invitation telling everyone to wear all black and to prepare their roast speeches beforehand.

5. Decorate the venue in black. Blow up pictures of the roastee (just like a funeral). Pick the most embarrassing pictures you can find (unlike a funeral).

6. Print out pamphlets with drinking quotes from that person, pictures, and a predetermined list of roasters.

7. The master of ceremonies should cap the roasting to two minutes per person.

8. After all the roasters have laced into the birthday boy, have the pallbearers carry him down to the nearest tavern. Proceed to celebrate Irish wake style. Car-bombs for everyone!

PLAYLIST

"Amazing Grace"
Dropkick Murphys

"Cadence to Arms"
Dropkick Murphys

"Finnegan's Wake"
Dropkick Murphys

"I'm Shipping Up to Boston"
Dropkick Murphys (*The Departed* theme song)

"Alcohol"
Gogol Bordello

"Drunken Lullabies"
Flogging Molly

"Tobacco Island"
Flogging Molly

"These Exiled Years"
Flogging Molly

"Selfish Man"
Flogging Molly

"Salty Dog"
Flogging Molly

"The Likes of You Again"
Flogging Molly

"If I Ever Leave This World Alive"
Flogging Molly

"Whiskey, You're the Devil"
The Clancy Brothers

"Whiskey in the Jar"
The Dubliners

Any song by The Pogues

FLIP CAMERA FILM FEST

Plan your own Academy Awards ceremony . . . only with less special effects, and more red wine. This daylong event assigns participants to competing film crews. Each team has to use a flip camera (*www.theflip.com*) to shoot and edit a three-minute montage movie.

THE SET-UP

The real Oscars are clearly won by manning eighteen-hour shifts on the receiving end of a glory hole. There is no other explanation as to how Clint Eastwood channeled every American grandfather in his *Gran Torino* performance and still lost to Sean "Whip Cream Tickle" Penn in *Milk*. (5th Year actually heard from a reliable source that Eastwood has melted down his many Oscars and turned them into bullets. These bullets are used to kill mythical female sea beasts that he in turn sucks the blood from guaranteeing him longer life and increased longevity in the bedroom. He keeps gold-painted steel versions of the award in his house to fool John Q. Public.) Anyways, our contest is judged on the actual ancient art of talent. Follow these rules and judge teams on their ability to get creative within the set parameters.

1. Each team will have five members: lead male, supporting male, lead female, supporting female, and one director/editor (feel free to have cameos).
2. Every film will have the same storyline: Guy loses girl, but after a mantage, guy wins girl back.

Mantage: It's like a montage, only it's a bunch of clips that show the protagonist becoming more manly.

3. Films must be submitted before 8 P.M.
4. Contestants will vote for winners in each category.
5. Each winner gets to give a short acceptance speech to the audience.
6. Make sure your master of ceremonies has Scotch in hand the whole time—just like Robert Goooooulet!

And may the best mantage win.

OVER THE TOP

If you really want to go the Academy Awards route, rent out a banquet facility or the back room of an Italian restaurant. You can even set up a red carpet entrance and have the master of ceremonies interview guests as they arrive. If you do it on an off-night, you can probably work a deal with the place to do a cheap buffet-style meal and reasonable corkage fee.

DRESS THE PART

Make the stars and get done up for the big event.

Guys: Ugly suits and tuxedos are encouraged.

Girls: Cocktail dresses, swanky evening gowns, big hairdos, and an excessive amount of gaudy jewelry. Prepare your acceptance speeches beforehand.

Award Categories

Best Actor

Best Supporting Actor

Best Actress

Best Supporting Actress

Best Director

Best Kiss

Best Screenplay

Lifetime Achievement Award

Best Film

THE GORDON GECKO DINNER PARTY

It's all about the many Ss of *success*. The formula for is simple:

Slickbacks + Suits + Suspenders + Scotch + Steak = Gordon Gecko

Lunch is for wimps, greed is good, and the only thing that beats a bloody porterhouse is bankrupting your enemies. It's time to blow off a long week of selling stocks (playing Brickbreaker in your cubicle).

THE SET-UP

You and your fellow i-bankers (telemarketers) are out to celebrate the closing of the Lieberman account (excuse to get away from girlfriends for one night). Pick a steakhouse and invite some of your peers—not *friends*, if you need a friend get a dog. Spend the night trying to establish the alpha male at the table by sharing tales of exploiting ugly, poor people. Here are a few activities that will keep you millionaires busy . . .

Empty Threats Challenge

After the first Scotch is increasing the level of your assholiness, give each dinner attendee a note card and a pen. It's time to learn some Sun Tzu negotiation skills: "If you can't convince your enemy to take the deal make up unbelievable threats against his family." Each player writes down a funny phone threat on the card, turns it over, and slides it to the person on their right. Take turns reading each other's threats. If you laugh, you have to walk up to the bar and buy that person a Scotch.

Here are some good examples:

"Oh, ya? I'm going to land my helicopter on the four-square court of your son's elementary school, walk into his classroom, squat over his desk, and take a giant sushi shit right on top of it. Sign this deal!"

"Listen to me you simple, state-school-educated fuck! If you don't sign this deal, I am going to decapitate you with my cock and bury your body in the Atlantic. Then I am going to use your hollowed out skull as a birdhouse for my Peruvian parrots!"

"Gut check time, pussy! Do you have the stones or did Mommy stick her fingie too far up your poophole? Sign the fucking deal."

"Now, I said I would be nice, and I lied, because I'm a fucking pussy fucker, and you prefer greasy butt-holes. I end people. Fact. I love Stalin, 'cause he got the job done when shit needed to get done and he sure as shit wouldn't have tolerated a dick-fingering pole-smoker like you . . . consider yourself finished in this town. Now get me a protein shake, being around such an immense black hole of pussiness has lowered my sperm count."

I Gotta Hot Tip

Have each i-banker chip in so that you have a stack of one hundred ones. Place it on the table and tell the waitress that every time she screws up, you're going to take a dollar of the top. Give her the remaining amount and leave her with your business card for Prestige Worldwide.

Credit Card Roulette

It's time to settle the bill. Put all the attendees credit cards into a dinner napkin and shake it up. Have the waitress pull out half of the cards. Those lucky bastards get to split the bill and the others get to save it for their bail money when they get arrested for insider training. In the immortal words of Gordon Gecko, "What's worth doing is worth doing for money."

HALLOW-THANK-MAS EVE

Halloween kicks off the holiday season. Most college students and young adults are forced into family obligations and don't get to celebrate the holidays with the people they really love—their friends. Hallow-Thank-Mas Eve combines the awesomeness of all these celebrations.

THE SET-UP

This dinner party requires people to dress in Halloween costumes, eat a Thanksgiving meal, and do Kris Kringles while celebrating New Year's Eve . . . all in one jam-packed night. The host of the party should pick a nice fall day and send out an invitation telling people to wash their beer-stained Halloween costumes. Once people have confirmed, randomly assign Kris Kringles and cap the spending limit at $10. You can say the gift has to start with the same letter as the person's name. After your dinner, have a silent vote (via paper ballot) for the best costume. The winner gets a white Russian Christmas gift basket (Kahlua, vodka, and warm milk) and chooses the kickass after dinner drinking games.

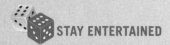

STAY ENTERTAINED

Nothing says holiday like some wholesome binge drinking. Write each of these twenty-seven rules on two Jenga blocks (there are fifty-four blocks total). The person to topple the Jenga tower has to take a slap shot (taking a shot with a slap to the face as the chaser).

1. Have your own Pants-Off Dance-Off.

2. Pinch your own nipples until it's your turn again.

3. Slap Shot!

4. Bust a rhyme. (First person to screw up the rhyme loses and takes a drink.)

5. Sing the chorus of your favorite Disney song.

6. Eat a spoonful of mayo.

7. Truth or Dare (Pick a player of your choice.)

8. Call the last person you hooked up.

9. Take off your shirt, draw a face on your stomach, and put a cigarette in your bellybutton.

10. High Fives All Around!

11. Pick a partner and finish your beers.

12. Try to Moonwalk.

13. Categories! (First person who can't think of something that falls within the assigned category loses and has to take a drink.)

14. Give out five drinks.

15. Do a recording on the T-Pain iPhone app.

16. Piggyback Ride! (Hop on another player's back and finish your beer.)

17. Yell "penis" as loud as you can.

18. Take your shirt off and get a pink belly from the player to your left.

19. Get a wine-cork moustache (burn an end of a cork with a lighter and use it as charcoal pencil to make a moustache).

20. Bend over and get spanked by the player of your choice.

21. Pick two people to thumb wrestle. (Loser takes five drinks.)

22. Start to "air masturbate." The last person to join in loses and has to take a drink.

23. Choose one person to chug a beer and choose another person whose face the chugger has to burp in.

24. Take a shot out of someone's bellybutton.

25. Take off one piece of clothing for the whole game.

26. Pick someone to take off a piece of clothing for the whole game.

27. Give a magic marker arm tattoo to a player of your choice.

INSOMNIAC PHOTO HUNT

Cops, hookers, catching raccoons, and public urination . . . the Insomniac Photo Hunt makes for an adventurous activity you can do with your friends any night of the week. This scavenger hunt happens between the hours of 3 A.M. and 5 A.M. You have two hours to find the weirdest people and get into the strangest situations while documenting them all with a still camera.

THE SET-UP

Split four to eight friends into teams of two or three. It's important to have no more than three people on each team (having more than that will draw attention and limit your access) and you need at least two since the buddy system is vital when dealing with the trannies and crackheads of the night (who else would take the photo?).

Hand out the list of photos to create, review with both teams to discuss any discrepancies on the list . . . and go. Each photo is worth a predetermined amount

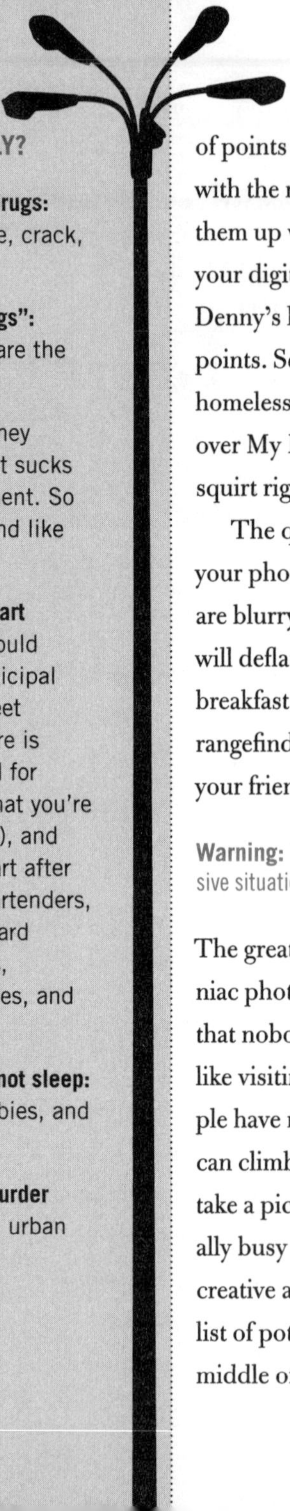

WHO'S AWAKE THIS EARLY?

People doing amphetamine drugs: Cocaine, methamphetamine, crack, speed, Dexedrine, etc.

People doing "Euro Club Drugs": Ecstasy and MDMA (those are the normal ones).

People who are homeless: They don't really sleep because it sucks sleeping on the cold pavement. So they could be walking around like zombies at 4 A.M.

People who have jobs that start after 2 A.M.: These people could work in factories or do municipal work like garbage men, street cleaners, nurses, cops (there is a chance you'll get arrested for something—just explain what you're doing and they'll let you go), and firemen. Other jobs that start after 2 A.M. include after-hour bartenders, strippers, hookers, illegal card house dealers, dockworkers, underground fighting referees, and bakery workers.

People who legitimately cannot sleep: Insomniacs, old people, babies, and new moms.

People who are looking to murder other people: This is just an urban legend, or is it?

of points based on difficulty. The team with the most points and photos to back them up wins the competition. Compare your digital photos at a predetermined Denny's location at 5:30 A.M. Tally the points. Seeing your friend spooning a homeless man should make the Moons over My Hammy plastic Velveeta cheese squirt right through your nose.

The quality and composition of your photos are crucial. If your pictures are blurry or are just plain boring, it will deflate the potential greatness of breakfast. Make sure what you see in the rangefinder is a worthy picture to show your friends.

Warning: You may encounter strange and aggressive situations between the hours of 3 to 5 A.M.

The great thing about doing an insomniac photo hunt is that you get pictures that nobody has ever seen. It's kind of like visiting a foreign country. Most people have never been out that late. You can climb light posts, high-five hookers, take a picture in the middle of a usually busy road, and the list goes on. Get creative and let the flash fly. Here is a list of potential activities to shoot in the middle of the night.

List of Hunting Items (1–5 points)

- ❑ Spoon a homeless man while he is sleeping (4 points)
- ❑ Slow dance with a hooker (3 points)
- ❑ Slow dance with a tranny (5 points)
- ❑ Get handcuffed by a cop (4 points)
- ❑ Ride on a fire truck (3 points)
- ❑ Ride a garbage truck (2 points)
- ❑ Ride a bus (1 point)
- ❑ Eat half a dozen donuts (2 points)
- ❑ Find the most inexpensive meal and eat it (3 points)
- ❑ Print your butt at a twenty-four hour Kinko's (4 points)
- ❑ Swim in a hotel swimming pool (3 points)
- ❑ Catch an animal (3 points)
- ❑ Climb a streetlight (2 points)
- ❑ Enter an abandoned building (2 points)
- ❑ Streak a famous street (4 points)
- ❑ Shave in a public bathroom (2 points)
- ❑ Get yelled at by someone in an apartment building (4 points)
- ❑ Sell something at a pawnshop (2 points)
- ❑ Ride an electric cart at an all night grocery store (2 points)
- ❑ Have your smallest teammate squeeze into a laundry mat dryer (2 points)
- ❑ Shotgun a 16-ounce Red Bull (1 point)
- ❑ High five a 7-Eleven employee (1 point)
- ❑ Take a picture with the cook at an all-night Chinese restaurant (2 points)
- ❑ Ding-dong ditch a friend's house (1 point)
- ❑ Take a man-gyna photo in front of a famous city landmark (3 points)
- ❑ Use fake money to take a "make it rain" picture outside a strip club (3 points)
- ❑ Take a team picture in paper Burger King crowns (2 points)
- ❑ Draw a moustache on a realtor's bus bench advertisement (3 points)
- ❑ Find a public bathroom and write a competitor's name and phone number on a wall with a sexual proposition like, "For a good time call . . ." (1 point)
- ❑ Eat a Denny's $2.99 Grand Slam (2 points)
- ❑ Recreate the Beatles' *Abbey Road* album cover (1 point)
- ❑ Capture your teammates mid-air as they jump in front of a brick wall (1 point)
- ❑ Sneak onto a football field and pose as a quarterback and offensive line (3 points).

IT'S JARTY TIME!

Jeans + Party = Jarty

Are you ready to cream in your jeans at this all-denim extravaganza? Acid-washed Daisy Dukes and Canadian tuxedos? Hey oh! Don't bring that country club khaki to this shindig or Springsteen himself will chloroform you with the working-class sweat from his red bandana.

THE SET-UP

The Jarty forces friends to get creative with their jean costumes. Here are some 5th Year suggestions:

Jirate: Tight jeans/vest, pirate tattoos, and eye patch
Jion, Jiger, and Jears: Denim clothes with animal (lion, tiger and bear) face paint
Jeagle: A bald eagle in kickass all-American jeans (wings required)
Jinja: Jean Jacket Ninja clans most commonly scene in Ninja Turtle movies

Jitch: The black jean version of the most popular Halloween costume (witch)
Jastronauts: Levis don't wrinkle in anti-gravity (fact and cool commercial)
Jalien: Aliens only abduct hillbillies so it makes sense they brought back this fashion
Juperman: Daisy Dukes over tight red jeans with a denim cape, and don't forget the "J" on the chest
Jimp: Keep the bling but substitute polyester for denim

Gone in Sixty Minutes: DJ Competition

Alright my jort (jean-short) sporting binge drinkers, it's DJ Duckbutter here from PopCrap 98.1! Don't let some Osama Spin Laden ruin your Jarty Time by playing bad Arab pop. Here's a surefire way to make sure you sweat through that denim.

Prior to your Jarty, have six friends pick which hour of the party they are going to DJ. Say your party starts at 1 P.M., write down the six-hour slots (1 P.M. to 2 P.M., 2 P.M. to 3 P.M., 3 P.M. to 4 P.M., and so on) and put them into a hat. Whichever slot that person pulls, they are responsible to DJ for that hour. All competing DJs should make their Canadian-superstar playlists prior to the event so there is no lull in the music.

There is no way in hell that any of your friends will be sober enough to vote at the end of the night. So the judging should actually be done by the DJs themselves. Each DJ should pick which of the spinners they competed against rocked the Canuck music the hardest.

Rules

1. All the music each competing DJ uses in their playlists must have some tie to the Great White North.
2. *Wedding Singer*–style microphone work, side games, and props are mandatory.
3. If you catch a DJ playing a song that's already been played make them drink.
4. The hipsteriffic DJ trend is to conceal your face with a mask (be it hockey, Spiderman, robot helmet, or Mexican wrestling mask). It's not mandatory, but it should be strongly encouraged.
5. All DJ switches are done at the top of the hour. If they go over their time, they are disqualified from the competition.

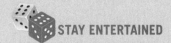

STAY ENTERTAINED

Keep the Canadian thing going when it comes to choosing an activity to enjoy during your denim festivities. Get the party going with one of these two Canuck favorites.

HOCKEY: The Drinking Game

The problem with real hockey is that you have to play on skates (tough) or roller blades (gay). Take out the shitty stuff so you can focus on the scoring and the drinking. Hockey: The Drinking Game is a stand-up drinking game best played around a big table or kitchen island. The game must be played with glass bottles or coffee mugs.

Everyone stands shoulder distance apart from each other with their bottles directly in front of them on the table. The game starts with the selected player spinning the quarter on the table so it is somewhere near the center of the rink. While the quarter is still spinning, the selected player yells out someone's name. That person has to quickly try and slap the spinning quarter into someone's beer bottle/can or glass. The hitting techniques vary from the backhand, chip shot, forehand, reflick, or the reach around. As soon as someone's name is called, every other player can use two fingers (most people use the pinky index combo) to block the shot. This is called your goalie.

The Rules

1. If your cup gets hit before you can react, you must adhere to the drinking penalty. The person who scores the goal spins the quarter on the table and then the whole table has to try and keep it spinning. This can be done by lightly "reflicking" the quarter in the same direction. While the quarter is spinning, the person who was just scored on must keep drinking. Sometimes these penalties can go on for a long time and other times the quarter will spin right off the table.

2. If someone is starting a round and spins the quarter off the table, the player is in the penalty box. This means you are not allowed to block your goal (cup) for one round. You are now an open goal and will most likely get scored on again.

3. If someone blocks the quarter with their hand and not their fingers, that person is in the penalty box and cannot block his beer in the next round.

4. If a person goes to hit/block but knocks over a beer, they are in the penalty box. Bring in the Zamboni (paper towels) to clean up their mess.

5. If a beer bottle gets hit but the quarter continues to spin on the table, the puck is still live. A live puck can be played by anyone. A puck is always live until it is laying flat. Multiple goal scores on one person equal multiple drinking penalties.

MOOSE! The National Canadian Drinking Game

Moose is a simple drinking game played with a quarter and an empty ice tray. (Sporting a Canadian tuxedo and ending every sentence with "eh" won't improve your play, but it can help psych out the competition.)

The Rules

1. Contestants take turns bouncing the quarter into the tray. The left side of the tray is for L-O-S-E-R Penalties and right side of the tray is R-E-W-A-R-D-S.

2. If a player sinks a quarter into the last slot on the ice tray (left or right) every player has to yell the word "Moose," put their thumbs to their head, and make their hands look like moose antlers. The last player to make a moose formation has to finish their entire drink.

3. If you miss the tray entirely, you drink for three seconds.

R1: Give out three seconds of drinking to player of choice.

R2: Give out five seconds of drinking to player of choice.

R3: The two people to your left or right have to intertwine arms and drink for five seconds.

R4: Give a wet willie/noogie/wedgie to a player of your choice.

R5: Waterfall starting with you.

R6: Make a rule for the table (Examples: No first names, pointing, swearing or you have to end every sentence with the word "fetus.")

R7: MOOSE!

L1: You drink for three seconds.

L2: You drink for five seconds.

L3: You have to pinch your own nipples until it's your turn again (or thumb in mouth, forehead on table, blindfolded or continuously dancing).

L4: The person to the right of you gets to give you a wet willie/noogie/wedgie.

L5: Waterfall ending with you.

L6: The person to your left makes a rule involving you.

L7: MOOSE!

LAST-MINUTE HALLOWEEN

Halloween is one of those holidays that the 5th Year tends to avoid. It's the one day of the year people let their guard down and put on a funny outfit. Really though, if everyone is dressed up in a creative costume at the same time, doesn't that make it not creative anymore? A great anti-activity to plan is a Last-Minute Halloween. Avoid the pressure of a perfect costume and crowded lines . . . just wing it.

THE SET-UP

Get your friends to show up at your house at a predetermined time in regular clothing. Arrange transportation (school bus is our favorite choice) and fill it up with your group and some ice-cold Zimas. Head to the nearest costume shop or thrift store. Once you arrive, everyone has exactly thirty minutes to have their costume on their backs, paid for, and back on the bus. Map out a series of bars to hit, pub-crawl style. Plan your pub crawl from 7 P.M. to 10 P.M., followed by a kickass house party.

KING'S CUP: 5TH YEAR REMIX

One way to keep things going during your Last-Minute Halloween is to start a game that can be put together at the last minute—like Kings. The hardest thing about Kings is deciding which set of rules you're going to use since everyone has a somewhat different version. So we've settled it for you. Here's the 5th Year Remix:

Ace: To Someone Else's Face—as soon as an Ace is pulled the last person to have their hand on someone else's face has to drink.
2: To You—the person who pulls the card gets to pick someone to drink.
3: To Me—the person who pulls the card has to drink.
4: To the Floor—the last person with their head on the table drinks.
5: To the Sky—the last Person with their hands in the air drinks.
6: Girls get to pick a camera pose for the guys. (Try to keep it hetero.)
7: Guys get to pick a camera pose for the girls. (No comment.)
8: Pick a Mate—for a waterfall, where the two of you start drinking and the other can't stop until you do.
9: Bust a Rhyme—the person who pulls the card says a sentence then the person to his left must say a sentence that ends with a word that rhymes with the last word of the previous sentence. This continues until someone can't come up with a rhyme. (It's a 5th Year favorite.)
10: Rules—the person who pulls the card gets to make a rule that lasts for the rest of the game.

Fun Rules

A. No pointing, no swearing, or no first names.
B. Anytime anyone talks you have to end your statement with one of these words: dildo, badonkadonk, bacon dick, fetus, guacamole, moist panties, or muffin tops.
C. The last person who pulled a 10 (or the next one who does if no one else has) must continue to play with two ping-pong balls in their cheeks until another 10 is pulled.
D. Every person to pull a 6 has to fake an orgasm.
E. Pick an accent that the whole table must use until another 10 is pulled. Anyone out of character has to drink.

Jack: Categories—the person who pulls the card chooses a category then, starting with the player to the left, everyone has to say someone or something that fits in that category. The first person who can't think of something or repeats an answer has to drink.

Fun Ideas

Items in a Brown Bag Lunch, Simpsons Characters, Old White Lady Names.

Queen: Questions—the player who pulls the card asks someone a question and then that person must ask someone else a question, and so on. The first one to laugh, answer the question they've been asked, or hesitate has to drink.
King: King's Cup—the player who pulls the card pours a decent amount of whatever he is drinking into the King's Cup located in the center of the table. When the fourth King is pulled, the person who chose it has to chug the King's Cup.

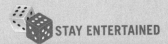

STAY ENTERTAINED

What's scarier than taking your own fate in your hands? To add some extra fright to your Last-Minute Halloween, have partygoers participate in the Dice Game. Here's the 5th Year's take on getting drunk with dice:

1. When it's your turn you simply call out someone's name, pick a number on the die, and make a demand. For example: "If I roll a four, McLovin has to stand in front of the group and karaoke Meatloaf's 'I Would Do Anything for Love.'"

2. If the number is rolled, the person has to comply with the demand or opt out with a shot.

3. A person cannot be selected twice in a row and can only opt out with a shot three times. Consider the shots like *Monopoly*'s Get Out of Jail Free cards.

4. The die is then passed clockwise and the next person gets to make a demand. The game always ends up with drunk a-holes trying to get girls to make out, but look below for some creative demands we've come up with:

If I roll a two you have to . . .

MILD

Fake an orgasm in the Chewbacca voice.

Go into a closet with a girl and switch clothes.

Hold two ping-pong balls in your mouth until a selected number is rolled.

Slap yourself in the face as hard as you can.

Eat a spoonful of mayonnaise.

WILD

Take a fart cup. (Someone farts into a keg cup and you must put it over your nose and mouth, and then inhale.)

Make yourself puke. Go ahead—pull the trigger.

Wear your coin purse out of your jeans until a selected number is rolled.

Snort a line of salt.

Have another contestant go to the refrigerator and pollute his or her breath with as many foul items as possible then breathe directly into your mouth and nose.

LEPRECHAUN EXTRAVAGANZA

Imagine your shortest friend (preferably a ginger) painted gold from head to toe. He's wearing rollerblades and he is pumping his legs for dear life. Why? Because there's a pack of carnivorous drunkees chasing him down with one thing on their mind—capture that leprechaun. However, in order to catch the leprechaun, you must achieve hunting rights, earned by winning a number of drinking games prior to the race.

THE SET-UP

The Extravaganza is a kickass party with a flash mob twist (inspired by our friends, Mattimeo and Ace Frehley, from UC Davis).

Two keys to the Leprechaun Extravaganza are picking the right leprechaun (make sure he is good on rollerblades) and having a great racecourse picked out (a college campus is ideal). After the games have been played and pole positions are determined, the leprechaun should get a few minutes head start. The host then releases the teams according to where they placed in the drinking games. Imagine a stampede of green clad maniacs chasing down a leprechaun like a hunt on the Serengeti. The team to catch him wins the Pot O'Goldschlager trophy!

The Games

Separate partygoers into coed teams of four for a series of drinking games. Scoring: three points for a first place finish, two points for second, and one point for third.

Car Bomb Beer Pong: This is the Irish version of Battleship beer pong. Set up a four by four square of beer pong cups. Each team hides four Irish car bombs in the sixteen-cup grid. The first team to get all the car bombs (not all the cups) wins the match. Organize a two-table bracket and keep the games moving quickly.

Beer Darts: See the Beer Olympics entry for rules.

Corn-hole Tournament: Corn-hole is a lawn game where players toss beanbags onto a plywood platform that has a hole in the center. Visit its Wikipedia page for the official rules, scoring, and to learn how to build your own set of corn-hole platforms.

Survivor Flip Cup: Have two teams line up on opposite sides of the table. Use red plastic cups, and fill them up about a quarter of the way. Start with the ends, and have opposing players "cheers" each other, tap their cup to the table, then chug. After the beer is done, the player must flip his cup from upright position to upside down position. Once he lands this flip, the next man on the line can start chugging. So forth and so on. Now for the "Survivor" part. After each round, a player gets voted off of the team from the opposing team. Best players are usually voted off first.

Anchorman: See the Beer Olympics entry for rules.

Line the teams up in the order of beer games rank. Let the first team loose with a minute head-start and then release teams every thirty seconds in the order they finished. Make sure to text the leprechaun a warning Paul Revere style, "The ~~English~~ Drinkers are coming!"

LITTLE LEAGUE DINNER BET

During a 5th Year slosh-ball game a few years back, a neighboring field was chockfull of preschoolers. They were organizing an intense relay race. Our game of slosh-ball became insignificant when we saw these kids running, tripping, falling, and finishing their races. Without very much discussion, we started picking kids and betting on them, like they were greyhounds at the track. You just never know who's going to pull it out with kids, which makes them great for making all kinds of wagers. This was the moment it happened and the Little League Dinner Bet was born.

THE SET-UP

Gather an even number of friends and find a Little League game. Split your friends in two groups. Each group gets one Little League team. The group with the losing Little League team has to buy the winners dinner. Keep it mildly classy. Don't pull a *Good Will Hunting* and heckle with brown-bagged forties. If you win, feel free to order extra appetizers, 'cause you're not paying for this one.

PLAY FOR PRIDE

In college, we loved gambling but only had enough money for frozen burritos and Winner's Cup Vodka. Save the $56 in your bank account and put your dignity on the line instead. Rather than taking the winners out for dinner, take the losers' respect.

"Friendly" Wagers

- Losers have to get their bellybuttons pierced and wear the rings for one month.
- Losers get videotaped singing *Aladdin*'s "A Whole New World" and it gets uploaded to Facebook.
- Winners get to dress and pose the Losers in any items found in the house and the pictures get posted on Facebook.
- Winners get to dictate a letter that the Losers have to e-mail to their mothers and grandmothers, explaining how they are coming out of the closet.
- Losers have to smoke a whole cigarette through their noses.
- Losers have to take a man-gyna picture that gets e-mail blasted to friends.
- Losers have to get spray-on tans done with Playboy Bunny stickers on their chests.
- Losers have to walk to the nearest convenient store with "cock" written on their foreheads and buy condoms.
- Losers have to walk into a Jamba Juice, order smoothies, and pour them down their pants inside the store.
- Losers have to go to a nice sit-down dinner, with blow-up dolls as each of their dates.
- Winners get to give the Losers a haircut of their choice. Losers must keep it for twenty-four hours.
- Losers have to go see a movie of the Winner's choice in an outfit also of their choice.
- Losers must walk through the local mall in spandex workout gear with a boom box that is blasting Olivia Newton-John's "Let's Get Physical."
- Each winner gets to pick a Fathead sticker for one of the Losers that they must buy and keep up in their bedrooms for one month.
- Winners get to pick a Watch Instantly television show from Netflix and the Losers have to watch the entire season.
- Losers have to Nair their chest and armpit hair.
- Winners get to create the voicemail messages for all the Losers, who must keep it that way for one month.
- Losers have to read Spencer Pratt and Heidi Montag's book *How to Become Famous*. And write a book report.
- Winners make the Losers panhandle for one full hour on the street of their choice with signs of their choice.
- Winners get to create a personal ad for each Loser and then post it on Craiglist with their picture.

MASHUP DINNER PARTY

We all owe thanks to the first stoner who accidentally played Pink Floyd's *Dark Side of the Moon* in sync with *The Wizard of Oz*. In his face-melting moment of discovery, he could have never imagined the huge web culture that would develop around mashups.

Most often, a mashup is a "composition created by blending two or more songs, usually by overlaying the vocal track of one song seamlessly over the music track of another" (according to Wikipedia). However, mashups aren't limited to just music. They've become popular for web applications (TwitterMap) and movie trailers (*Scar Wars* and *Brokeback to the Future*).

Mixing unlikely combinations whilst under the influence sounds like a great idea so let's take this concept and turn it into a dinner party.

THE SET-UP

All attendees are required to bring one strangely delicious food combination. For inspiration, check stoner forums or go to *www.ThisIsWhyYoure Fat.com*.

Food Ideas

- *Chocolate chips in buttered popcorn*
- *Peanut butter apple slices*
- *Grilled cheese with pears, mayo, and alfalfa sprout sandwiches*
- *Potato chips dipped into sour cream that's mixed with hot sauce*
- *Peanut butter and aged swiss on nilla wafers*
- *Mac and cheese/baked bean burritos*
- *Cream cheese bacon bagel*
- *Cinnamon cream cheese celery sticks*
- *Eggo waffle ice cream sandwich*
- *White-trash nachos (Kraft singles melted over ruffles)*
- *Cheetos in chicken noodle soup*
- *Jack in the box monster tacos with ranch sauce*
- *Pancakes rolled with peanut butter and captain crunch*
- *French fries with melted mozzarella and brown gravy*
- *Tater tots with alfredo sauce*

All attendees are required to wear a mismatched set of clothing patterns. Pick any combination of polka dots, stripes, plaid, argyle, neon, tie-dye, silk, or leather. If your outfit requires a glass of wine to feel comfortable, you've got the right contrast.

The host should make a mashup playlist for the night and burn everyone a CD (or flash drive) with the songs. Here is a list of some of our favorite mashup websites:

- *www.bootiela.com*
- *www.looandplacido.com*
- *www.foxsounds.net (DJ Chris Fox)*
- *www.DJlobsterdust.com*
- *www.divideandkreate.com*

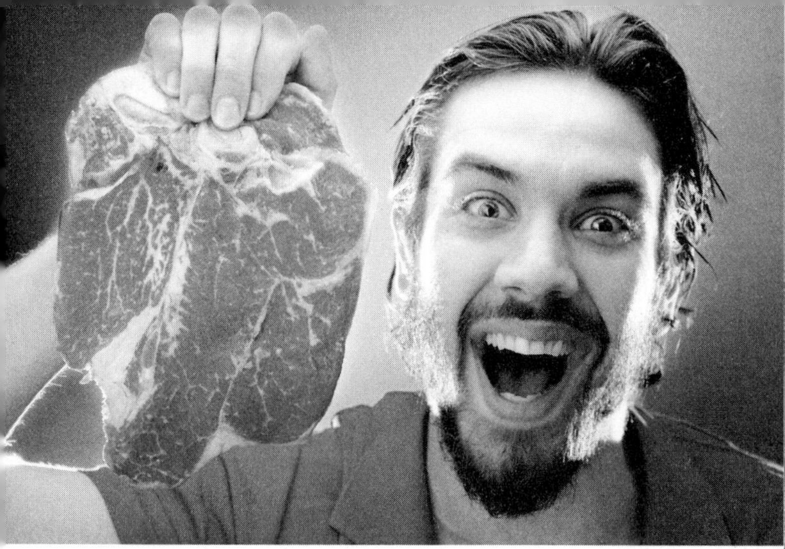

MEAT BABY!

Human sacrifice has pleased the gods for thousands of years. You want to end a drought? Chop some heads off. You want your crops to yield food? Chuck a few farmers off of a pyramid. Having trouble making babies? Sacrifice ten or twelve other people's babies. These are all logical steps to solving problems, right?

Meat Baby! is a dinner party to celebrate the almighty God of Meat. Meat, as we know, is the flesh of animals. Today, it's readily accessible at your corner Best Buy of Meat, or whatever. Years ago though, people had to actually catch their meat, kill it, and then eat it. So, when you risked your life to kill a wooly mammoth, it was a big fucking deal. Eating meat was reserved for special occasions. As is the sacrifice of the Meat Baby!

THE SET-UP

Diversity is important when preparing your Meat Baby. The Meat God prefers it. You must use a wide variety of store-bought meat products in order to craft the perfect Meat Baby. Ground beef is cheaper than bottled water these days. Thus, it serves as a great foundation in the construction of the Meat Baby. Layer your beef with other meat products (we'll get to that). Here is a suggested list of how to construct a Meat Baby. If you own a farm or hunt regularly, feel free to use local products to make your MB unique. This is America; nobody is telling you how to make your Meat Baby. Express yourself.

Head: Ground chicken
Eyes: Canadian bacon
Mouth: Applewood smoked bacon
Neck and Shoulders: Ground beef
Chest Plates: T-bone steaks
Sternum: NY strip steak
Arms: Ground lean turkey
Stomach: Ground beef
Belly button: Sliced hot dog
Hands: Pork chops
Pelvic girdle: Bacon diaper
Legs: Ground beef
Feet: Chorizo sausage

The party should resemble a sacrifice of the gods. Sacrificial activities include traditional dress, prayer, and song. Everyone should wear togas (made from bed sheets) and some kind of regal looking hat. A crown of bird feathers works really well. The more pre-Christian the better. Everyone stopped sacrificing around the time J-Dub came on the scene. Boo! So go old. Aztec's loved killing people for the gods and so did the ancient Egyptians (not modern Egyptians). Google image "Aztec" or "Ancient Egyptian" and you will find some costumes to emulate.

After you construct the sacrificial Meat Baby, march it to your grill in the traditional conga line. The participants should be singing songs of meat. We like to make up meat songs for this event. There just aren't many songs already written about meat and how great it is. (Business idea?) After the Meat Baby is sent to the fiery pits of sacrifice, the high priestess must bless the pile of flesh. The priestess should then offer the sacrifice to the God of Meat. Cook on high for at least forty-five minutes.

Make sure you are inviting the right people—I mean don't invite your PETA/vegan/animal-molester friends to this one . . . or do and see what happens. Up to you.

MEATHEAD MONDAY

Generally speaking, becoming a meathead should be avoided at all costs. But this dinner party requires you to "embrace the meat" and transform into a 'roid-raging, momma-loving, weightlifting loudmouth. Cradle the world of the meathead and the meat will show you respect. MM is a weekly gathering that is more like a training session with food than a well-prepared dinner party. You'll be bench-pressing terrified "smaht kids" in time for your nine-egg omelet.

THE SET-UP

The meathead is a patron of the rage-induced activities. Therefore, make sure you have something violent to watch. Mixed martial arts, boxing, or mafia movies are a good start. Remember to high-five and scream when something violent happens. The chest bump is also a great way to show that you really care about something.

At Meathead Mondays, another part of the entertainment experience is working out. Make sure you

DRESS THE PART

Let me tell you a question, pal! What is the standard issue meat wear? Listen up.

Wife Beaters: Any color. How else are you going to compare pectoral strength when you're lifting all those weights?

Gelled Hair: Gotta respect the hair. It should be groomed in a streamline fashion. The modern meathead keeps it "tight." Cement the hair into place. Remember, when you go to headbutt a weaker kid in a scrap, you don't want your hair getting in the way of a direct knock out. Keep that cut clean, bro!

Sweats: You should wear a pair of pants that you're able to do squat lunges comfortably in.

Nice Kicks: A true meathead wears athletic shoes all of the time, except in the steam room—where he wears his bacteria covered flip-flops. You should always keep a pair of athletic shoes on . . . you never know when some fucking poser will challenge you to a forty-yard dash.

have a curl bar and dumbbells to use while you are hanging out with your sexually questionable friends. Eating eggs and watching Pesci neck stab a goombah while doing bicep curls is proven to prevent lactic acid buildup. Fact.

Every meathead knows that it's all about getting the maximum protein into those muscles because protein builds the guns, and the guns get the ladies.

In preparation for Meathead Mondays, you will need some key items:

- *Have sixty eggs in your fridge at all times. You just never know.*
- *Go to Costco and buy the large packets of chicken breasts and a few packets of turkey meat.*
- *Always be stocked on canned tuna.*
- *Salad won't build biceps that intimidate "player haters." Forget the greens.*
- *Milk is a staple in the meathead diet. It comes from a cow tit, so it must be powerful stuff.*
- *Jugs of red wine should always be on hand. Meatheads are largely Italian, so having red wine with your chicken/turkey/tuna scramble is the only way to subdue your testosterone and prevent you from face punching your bros.*

5TH YEAR MONOPOLY

It's great how you can take a regular every day board game, like *Monopoly*, and turn it into a kick-ass drinking game. You could play *Candy Land* for hits of LSD, but Gloppy the Molasses Monster will never teach you about the cutthroat principles of American capitalism. That is why *Monopoly* is still the Mike Tyson of board games. Though of course, we've modified the original game with a hilarious combo of politically incorrect humor and binge drinking. Prepare for the rich to get drunk off of distilled liquor and the poor to get bombed off of brown bag forties. May the best monocle-clad industrialist win.

THE SET-UP

Each player chooses a deed card from the bin. Upon receiving the deed, that player is then relocated to his/her respective area of the room. Your team is determined by which color card you have chosen as teams are made up of the same colored properties (like Ventnor, Atlantic, and Marvin Gardens). Each team drinks and accessorizes according to the socioeconomic level of the card they have chosen. So, Baltic and Mediterranean deed holders will be drinking brown-bagged Steel Reserve in homeless attire while Boardwalk and Park Place will be enjoying the finer things in life like champagne, top hats, and monocles.

THE RAILROAD AND UTILITY DEEDS ARE UNION WORKER CARDS. THE PLAYERS WHO CHOOSE THESE DEEDS WILL HAVE A SPECIAL DUTY OF DECIDING WHICH PLAYER ON A TEAM HAS TO PERFORM THE TASKS CHOSEN FROM THE COMMUNITY CHEST AND CHANCE CARDS. (YES, THERE ARE COMMUNITY CHEST AND CHANCE CARDS.) THESE DELEGATE DIFFERENT DRINKING ACTIVITIES, ACTIONS, TRADES, AND PAYMENTS.

Monopoly Teams

PROPERTIES	TEAM THEME*	COSTUME	DRINK CHOICE
Baltic and Mediterranean	Hobos	Cutoff Gloves and beanies	Forties of Steel Reserve
Railroads and Utilities	Union Workers	Fake mustaches	Miller High Life
Oriental, Vermont, and Connecticut	Asian Immigrants	Pony tail and a skull cap	Tsingtao
Virginia, States, and St. Charles	Jamaicans	Rasta wigs and fake bling	Red Stripes
New York, Tennessee, and St. James	White Trash	Trucker hats, holding fake babies	Cans of Budweiser
Illinois, Indiana, and Kentucky	Hollywood Jews	Groucho glasses	Heineken Light
Marvin Gardens, Ventnor, and Atlantic	Mafia	Fedoras	Peroni
Pacific, North Carolina, and Pennsylvania	Southern Aristocrats	Barbershop quartet hats	Blue Moon beer
Boardwalk and Park Place	Rich Uncle Penny Bags	Top hats and monocles	Champagne

*Remember, this is the '20s. "Politically correct" has yet to be invented.

In the spirit of *Monopoly* and drinking, the black market is open. Capitalism will eventually prevail . . . and force your team into Challenge Matches for a chance at moving up or down the socioeconomic ladder. Caviar and champagne do not come easy, so be ruthless, and keep a watchful eye—through your monocle.

New and Improved Chance and Community Chest Cards

Ditch the standard issue deck and write all of these down on note cards.

Chance Cards

Team White Trash has another baby. Everyone else has to pay welfare by drinking for five seconds.

Mafia gets busted paying off Union. Union must vote one teammate to join the Hobos.

Hollywood Jews discovers Jamaican Team. The Hollywood team gets to pick one song for the Jamaicans to perform in front of everyone.

Union and Mafia get arrested for racketeering. Finish a six-pack in the bathroom jail.

Jamaicans demand reparations if they can roll an odd number on one try. If they do, they switch spots with the Southern Aristocrats.

Uncle Penny Bags raises taxes and starts a waterfall down the economic ladder.

Advance to Baltic Ave. Union Guys get to pick one of your teammates and one hobo. The hobo takes a swig of beer and burps in your face.

Cold winter! Hobos and Asians have to group hug for one whole round.

Loan matures. Pick one team to finish a yard glass of beer.

Life story gets optioned. Roll two dice and empty the amount into a beer yard. Hollywood Team has to finish the beer.

Countersue is successful! Banish one team to jail for one round.

News flash! Union Members caught sleeping on the job. They drink for seven seconds.

Congratulations! You win a lap dance from the Jamaicans.

Witness to Mafia murder! Your team picks one Mafia member to get spanked by the Union.

Inherit money to make movie. Pick one Hollywood member to act out a romantic sex scene and fake an orgasm.

Construction on house finished. Pick a Union member to finish a beer with your team.

Hollywood films outsourced! Pick an accent that the Hollywood team has to keep for one whole round.

Poor tax increases. Hollywood Jews, Mafia, Southern Aristocrats, and Rich Uncle Penny Bags drink together.

Your team takes stroll through Chinatown and gets complimentary shoulder massages from Asian team for one whole round.

News flash! White trash meth lab explodes! Shake one beer then group it with two others. Each White Trash teammate has to pick a can and open it under their nose.

Your team gets caught for tax evasion. Escape to Tijuana (bathroom) and turn the shower's hot water on for one round.

Prohibition passes. Pick one team that cannot drink for an entire round.

Advance to local burlesque show. Pick one female Southern Aristocrat to give your team a lap dance.

News flash! Religious revival swings through town! The next team to swear has to finish a yard glass.

News flash! Police wiretapping phones! Next team to use someone's first name has to finish a yard glass.

Get Out of Jail Free Card

Community Chest Cards

Race war erupts between Asians and Jamaicans. Each team gets thirty seconds to write down as many Wu Tang Clan members as possible. If the Asians win, they switch spots.

Hobos slept on Asians' doorstep. Fight erupts. Union members pick two female opponents to arm wrestle.

Jamaicans and White Trash get in argument over reggae vs. rock. Union picks song for air guitar showdown and votes on a winner.

Uncle Penny Bags and a Union Worker (of his choice) vs. two Southern Aristocrats in a beer chug

Gigli 2 *premieres. Hobos and Hollywood Jews get one minute to list as many Ben Affleck and Jennifer Lopez movies as possible. If Hobos win, they switch spots.*

The team closest to your position on the board picks one teammate and the Union Guys pick a person on your team to have a drink-off. The first one to finish their beer wins the challenge.

The team closest to your position on the board has thirty seconds to write down synonyms for penis. Your team has to write down synonyms for vagina. The team with the most wins.

IRS visits your house. If your team can successfully suck and blow a credit card down the line, you can switch positions with whichever team you want.

BLACK MARKET MONOPOLY

Want to go even wilder? Go straight cutthroat capitalism bitch! No rules on the black market. Buy, barter, bribe and seduce players with whatever you've got. Watch the unrelentingly gloomy system of exploitation unfold as the rich eventually wear everyone down. Even the nicest of friends will adopt Gordon Gecko's qualities in their rise to the top. Be careful of female guile. Is it worth it to give up Marvin Gardens for a breast grope?

McCONAUGHAVEN!

All right, all right, all right. When summer is in full swing, my amigos, it's time to get together for some good ol' fashioned day drinking. And with that, let's celebrate the one person who reminds us that "the older you get, the more rules they are going to try and get you to follow. You just gotta keep on livin', man. L-I-V-I-N." Of course, we are talking about the charming Texas Surfer Dude, Matthew David McConaughey.

THE SET-UP

McConaughey has gotten unfairly blasted by bloggy movie critics who have never created anything themselves. Is he the next Marlon Brando? Absolutely not, but the 5th Year has a theory on acting: The better the actor, the weirder the person. So the not-so great thespians are usually the people you would rather hang out with. For example, would you rather drink Nepalese tea with Johnny Depp while discussing the plight of the Native Americans? Or drive across the country in an Airstream while promoting *Sahara 2* with McConaughey, Penelope Cruz, and a cooler full of Miller Lites? The dude does cool shit. Give McConaughey the credit he deserves by throwing a party in his honor.

McConaugHaven Beer Pong Tournament for the J.K.L. (Just Keep Livin') Cup

- *All teams must have one girl and one guy.*
- *All players must be wearing a blonde wig and a bandana to enter the tournament.*
- *All teams must come up with a team name in relation to McConaughey's films, quotes, characters, or Texas (the Woodersons, The JKLs, The Saharans, Team Dazed, Team Confused, Surfer Dudes, Team I Love Them High School Girls, Team Miller Lyte (Matt's nephew's name), The Wedding Planners, Team Brazil, or Team I Love Them Redheads).*
- *Make two separate beer pong brackets: The Austin Bracket and the Malibu Bracket.*

DRESS THE PART

Girls: Daisy Dukes, Texas football shirts, Senior girl outfits from *Dazed and Confused*, Don't Mess With Texas shirts, and cowboy hats

Guys: Sarongs, Wooderson-style outfits from *Dazed and Confused*, or check out *www.cafepress.com* for a whole slew of McCona-themed shirts

STAY ENTERTAINED

Here are additional contests you can run:

McCona-Trivia (check his profile on *www.imdb.com* for good trivia)

McConaughey Impersonation Contest

Team Bongos Dance/Play Competition

Drunken Yoga Pose Competition

McCona-Pickup Line Competition (example: "Wanna drunk drive my Airstream cross-country and promote my new film, *Failure to Loose Fool's Gold in Ten Days*?)

MAKE SURE TO GET YOUR FILL OF THE McCONA-DIET OF CORONAS, PIÑA COLADAS, AND FISH TACOS.

THE TOP TWENTY MOVIE CHARACTERS WE WOULD WANT TO PARTY WITH

McConaughey's Wooderson makes the list. Check out who else we'd want on our dream guest list.

20. Ernie McCraken (Bill Murray) from *Kingpin*

Activity: Watch the National Bowling Championships at Hooters in Reno, Nevada while getting valuable life lessons from "Big Ern."

19. The Hanson Brothers (Jeff Carlson, Steve Carlson, and David Hanson) from *Slap Shot*

Activity: Eat two dozen hardboiled eggs. Proceed to finish a keg of Milwaukee's Best. Go to trendiest nightclub in town. Wear running shoes.

18. Lone Wolf McQuade (Chuck Norris) from *Lone Wolf McQuade*

Activity: Drunk mailbox bashing in McQuade's truck.

17. Jimmy (Chris Farley) from *Dirty Work*

Activity: Go on a dive-bar-to-Asian-massage-parlor romp while trying to find that damn Saigon whore!

16. Clubber Lang (Mr. T) from *Rocky III*

Activity: Drink a bottle of Jägermeister and take on the Princeton debate team, arguing in favor of global warming.

15. Floyd (Brad Pitt) from *True Romance*

Activity: Tray of brownies + '80s action movie marathon + delivery food = Great time

*Considered Tyler Durden from *Fight Club*, but the fact that Pitt turned down lead role in *True Romance* to play this character makes this choice worthy.

14. Wooderson (Matthew McConaughey) from *Dazed and Confused*

Activity: Go to a high school football game, talk about muscle cars, and scope out the new crop of girls.

13. Chet (Bill Paxton not Pullman) from *Weird Science*

Activity: Wear your old letterman jackets, go to an Emo concert, drink copious amounts of light beer, watch Chet give wedgies.

12. Al Czervik (Rodney Dangerfield) from *Caddyshack*

Activity: Wear plaid suits, bring six call girls to the nicest restaurant in town, and see how many people you can get to leave the establishment. Pick up their bill and insult the maître d' by throwing wads of cash in his face.

11. Trent Walker (Vince Vaughn) from *Swingers*

Activity: Ten hours in Vegas with $10,000.

10. Stephen (David O'Hara) from *Braveheart*

Activity: St. Patrick's Day in Boston carrying midgets dressed like leprechauns in baby backpacks while they lob potatoes at people in the parade.

9. Reed Rothchild, a.k.a. Chest Rockwell (John C. Reilly) from *Boogie Nights*

Activity: '70s Porn/Margarita/Magic Show/Pool Party at Jack Horner's

8. Stuart Mackenzie (Mike Meyers) from *So I Married an Axe Murderer*

Activity: Wake up 7 A.M. to watch Scottish football. Drink a bottle of Scotch and eat a pound of haggis. Go to Heed's "Bring Your Father to Class Day." Listen to Stuart's lecture on Scottish heritage. Leave in time for happy hour. Pull Heed out of class to drive.

7. Mickey the Pikey (Brad Pitt) from *Snatch*

ACTIVITY: Fly to Moscow and make shady deals on the black market. Drink barrels of vodka. Get more badass tattoos. Sleep with Mob bosses' daughters. Fight your way out.

6. Jake and Elwood (John Belushi and Dan Akroyd) from *The Blues Brothers*

ACTIVITY: Cross-country road trip stopping at every great rock star's grave to pay respects.

5. George Hanson (Jack Nicholson) from *Easy Rider*

ACTIVITY: Walk out of drunk tank at 7 A.M. Go to the nearest watering hole. Proceed to order red eyes (beer, raw egg, tomato juice). Shut bar down.

4. Jeff "The Dude" Lebowski (Jeff Bridges) from *The Big Lebowski*

ACTIVITY: Smoke leftover joints. Bowl a frame. Go to the steam room. Discuss philosophy. Pull $2,000 out of ATM. Visit Bunny.

3. Tie: Butch Cassidy, Cool Hand Luke, and Henry Gondorff (Paul Newman) from *Butch Cassidy and the Sundance Kid*, *Cool Hand Luke*, and *The Sting*

ACTIVITY: Escape from prison. Plan a heist. Retire to a tropical island with scantily clad women. Realize that the only evil in your life is your liver. Punish daily.

2. Randle Patrick McMurphy (Jack Nicholson) from *One Flew Over the Cuckoo's Nest*

ACTIVITY: Anything. He makes the best with what he has and makes sure everyone else is having a great time. Just like us.

1. Bluto Blutarsky (John Belushi) from *Animal House*

ACTIVITY: Hijack a window-washing elevator on a skyscraper. Drink two bottles of Jack Daniels. Lower to different floors and terrorize employees.

THE MILWAUKEE OPEN

Where the losers are more famous than the winners.

Announcer (whispering): It's the final hole. The Gene-Hack-Mans are tied with the Bunghole Putters for last place. It looks like he is sizing up the putt for the last time. This eight-footer is for all the marbles. He takes a practice swing. He is now addressing the ball and the putt is on its way . . . HE MISSED IT! HE MISSED IT! HE MISSED IT! HE HAS JUST WON HIMSELF A ONE-WAY BUS TICKET TO MILWAUKEE, WISCONSIN! THAT SUCKS.

When you and your friends have exhausted all other competitive activities, plan your own high stakes mini golf tournament. It's perfect for a birthday party, bachelor party, or fundraising event.

DRESS THE PART

All players are encouraged to wear colorful golf attire:

Plaid golf pants

Bright colored argyle sweaters

Knickers

High socks

Gatsby hats

Note: The losing team must wear their outfits onto the bus.

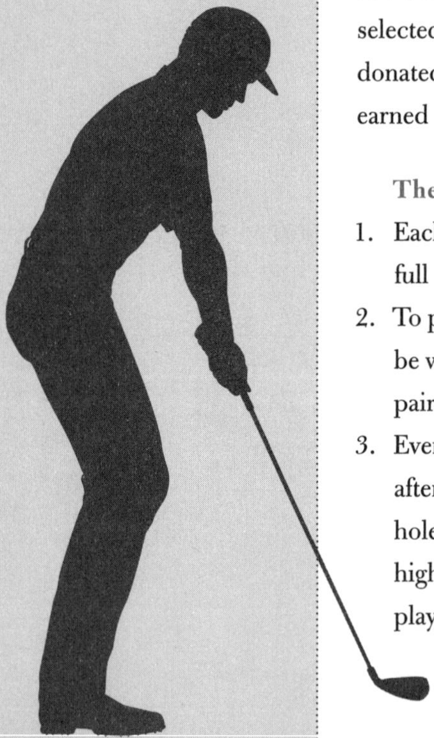

THE SET-UP

The Wager: Twosomes of mini golfers compete on a putt-putt course. The pair with the worst golf score is given one-way bus tickets and forced to get onboard directly after the competition.

Break into teams of two and have all of the players vote on a punishment city—preferably a town that's at least a day's drive. 5th Year and friends picked Milwaukee. The host should collect appropriate fees from each player and use them to buy two one-way Greyhound Bus tickets to the selected city. The rest of the money can be donated to a charity, or the guys that just earned a ride to Milwaukee.

The Rules

1. Each player is allowed one backpack full of toiletries and overnight clothes.
2. To prevent cheating, each hole should be watched/scored by another golfing pair.
3. Every stroke is counted as a point. If, after six strokes, the ball hasn't been holed, another point is added. The highest possible score for any hole and player is seven points.

4. Deliberate play to hit another's ball utilizing your own ball is allowed. However, deliberate striking of another's ball with your putter is *not* allowed.
5. When a ball comes to rest alongside or near to the perimeter boundary, or an obstacle, it can be repositioned (only by hand) up to eight inches at no penalty. Repositioning is to allow the player a proper back-swing and/or follow-through.
6. When a ball comes to rest in a ditch, bunker, or water hazard, it may either be played from where it lies (where the general repositioning rules apply) or, at a penalty of one stroke, it may be replaced on the green (in any direction) within eight inches of the ditch, bunker, or water hazard.
7. Golfers should play the first nine holes, take a lunch/beer break and then tally the scores before shooting the back nine.
8. The losing pair has to bring back visual documentation (pictures or video) that they visited the predetermined city. If you lose, make the most of it and bring back some good stories for your friends.

FUNNY GOLF TEAM NAMES

The Caddywhackers

The Blue Balls of Destiny

The One Hit Wonders

The Gene Hack-Mans

The Shooter McGavins

The Muff Burgers

The Bob Barkers

The Noonans

THE MOM JEANS AND DAD SWEATER PARTY

The day your parents had you, they stopped buying new clothes. They were too busy wiping your ass and feeding you to keep up with fashion. Their fashion time capsule, or clothes closet, therefore becomes a valuable asset and the perfect place to find inspiration for the Mom Jeans and Dad Sweater Party.

THE SET-UP

Wear your parents work clothes, or their causal hippie dipping duds. Your costume goals are simple: make everyone laugh. You'll need to raid your parents' closets for this party, so plan this over the holiday months when you and your friends are home from school. This party is great to throw at your parents' actual house, so try and convince your 'rents to switch pads to a hotel for a night. It can be your Christmas gift to them. If they tell you "absolutely not!", which most parents will say, then pick a dive bar to throw the party at. If you have your own place, do it there. Always pick party destinations that will allow you to take over the environment and make it your own. This is a very simple premise, easy to execute, and really no cost besides alcohol.

Make a House a Home

As you celebrate the awesomeness that is your parents' awkwardness, it's important to remember what they taught you about getting along as a family. In order to function under one roof, you needed to respect one another in order for things to work. The same is true for a good party house. You and your roommates need to respect one another in order to throw great parties.

Ten Rules for a Good Party House

1. All designated driver disputes are settled by *Mario Cart*. Last place has to drive.

2. After midnight, it is every man for themselves. Any complaints about selfish decisions (ninja vanishing with a girl, Jack in the Box runs, secret post-party hot tub ventures) will not be held up in a court of law.

Ninja Vanish: the act of drunkenly disappearing without telling anyone.

3. Roommates hold a monthly drinking game tournament and the winner gets to pick which roommate has to clean the pukie-pubes off the toilet.

4. Establish a "Ting Ting Jar." Any person who says something racist has to put one dollar in the jar. Proceeds go to pregame alcohol funds.

5. If you are responsible for bringing new people, you also get first choice on who you'd like to pursue. No poaching.

6. Roommates are allowed one Seabiscuit a month. A Seabiscuit is the act of withdrawing from a party to watch a movie with your girlfriend or boyfriend.

7. All friendly wagers must be documented by a third party so the loser has to go through with their punishments.

8. Roommates cannot be asked to lie to another roommate's significant other about his or her whereabouts.

9. Rides to the airport have to be requested at least two days in advance and a Subway sandwich is the proper reimbursement.

10. You break it you buy it.

PLAYLIST

End the night with the type of arm-in-arm, "I love you, man" drunken karaoke singalongs that old people love. Some good suggestions:

"Runaround Sue"
Dion

"Drift Away"
Dobie Gray

"Treat Her Right"
The Commitments

"Mellow Yellow"
Donovan

"Dance to the Music"
Sly and the Family Stone

"Build Me Up Buttercup"
The Foundations

"It's Not Unusual"
Tom Jones

"Can't Get Enough of Your Love, Babe"
Barry White

"Wonderful World"
Sam Cooke

"Ain't Too Proud to Beg"
The Temptations

"Twist and Shout"
The Isley Brothers

"Shout"
The Isley Brothers

"Soul Man"
Sam and Dave

"I Ain't Got Nobody"
Louis Prima

"Land of 1000 Dances"
Wilson Pickett

"Kokomo"
The Beach Boys

"Good Lovin'"
The Rascals

"Uptown Girl"
Billy Joel

"I'm a Believer"
The Monkees

"Coconut"
Harry Nilsson

MRS. ROBINSON PARTY

The cougar phenomenon is not a passing fad. Young girls are looking for financial security (which young men can't provide) and their biological clocks force them to apply commitment pressure (which scares the shit out of young men). Older women have been there, done that, and got a stack of cash from their last divorce settlement. Now they want someone with a sense of adventure and a sexual appetite to match. That's where you and your friends step in. There are hundreds of fun divorcees waiting for you to invite them to your Mrs. Robinson party.

THE SET-UP

Gather a group of your guy friends that are brave enough to approach older women. Each strapping bachelor is responsible to find and invite a date ten years his senior. Granted, it's not the easiest thing in the world to approach older women.

Here are some invite tips:

- *Unless you want to get punched in the face and have salt rubbed in your eyes, "Don't mow another man's lawn." Make sure she's not sporting a rock.*
- *Find the right hunting grounds—yoga class, health food store, happy hour at a nice restaurant or a martini bar.*
- *Don't be a scumbag and sling cheesy lines about ageless beauty. Be honest. "Look, my friends and I are having a Mrs. Robinson party. I have to find a date that's ten years older than me. No pressure, it's just an excuse for us to throw a fun party. If you're interested, I'd like you to come with me."*

Start with a fun dinner. Older women are stimulated by the art of conversation. Find a good BYOB restaurant, cheap margarita specials, or a good hole in the wall sake-bomb joint. Once people start to get boozed up, announce that you will be organizing speed dating. Pick one gender to stay stationary and the other to rotate. This sounds cheesy, but it's actually hilarious. This is a perfect chance to get to know everyone. Who knows, there might be a Sugar Momma willing to sponsor your keg art passion.

OVER THE TOP

For extra spice, have the host yell out different discussion topics for each round:

Your favorite non-Vegas party city in the U.S.?

What's your best New Year's Eve story?

Swap virginity-losing stories.

Cast an actor or actress in your partner's life story.

What is the one alcohol that's dangerous to you?

Greatest rock star of all time?

Favorite standup comedian?

Favorite movie about high school?

If you could sucker punch one celebrity, who'd it be?

After dinner, escort your Mrs. Robinsons to a good dive bar or karaoke spot. End the night with some good old-fashioned partying.

MY BIG FAT FAKE WEDDING

Everyone loves weddings. Free food, open bars, and frisky Aunt Karens. The only people not having fun are the ones saying, "*I do*." For everyone else, it's party time. What if you could have all the good stuff, without any of the hard stuff (like life-long commitment)? A *fake* wedding still equals a *real* party.

THE SET-UP

Treat this event like an actual wedding. The more detailed the plans, the more people will act like it's an actual ceremony. Seriously, we're talking invitations, a father/daughter dance, drunk speeches, the whole frickin' chalupa.

The host is charged with making a list of potential guests. You will need about thirty attendees to pull this wedding party off right. Anybody after that is considered a wedding crasher. The thirty main roles will either be delegated by the host, or randomly selected by the members, whichever you decide is easier.

Night One

Do a Power Hour. You can find some great mixes on *www.TheseArePowerfulHours.com*. A Power Hour will get everyone fired up and get people into character; any random guests will soon become friends.

AT ANY MULTIDAY EVENT, YOU'LL HAVE ACTIVITIES HAPPENING IN THE MORNINGS, AFTERNOONS, AND NIGHTS. WE KNOW YOU'LL BE HUNGOVER, BUT YOU NEED TO WAKE UP, HAVE A BLOODY MARY, TURN ON SOME MICHAEL JACKSON, AND KEEP THE PARTY GOING.

Night Two

Separate bachelor and bachelorette parties. Guys should arrange for small-town strippers to come and give mustache rides (Google it). The girls can mold clay penises and drink champagne in lingerie.

Day Three

Make the wedding a truly magnificent experience. Include the following:

- *The bride's walk up the isle*
- *A groom side and bride side for seating*
- *Flower girl (who should carry a basket full of Natural Lights)*
- *A drunken sermon from priest*
- *Floral arrangements inside of beer cans*
- *The bouquet and garter toss*
- *Speeches from the father of the bride and best man*
- *A father/daughter dance*

The amount of detail added to the ceremony will create a realistic feeling, leading to more tears, sloppy makeouts, and actual engagement proposals.

Set up a **reality show confessional booth.** Put a couch inside a linen closet and tape down a camcorder on a tripod. Guests are free to record whatever, whenever. You will end up with sloppy hookups, inanimate mumbling, and tons of blackmail.

Wedding Role-Play

THE GENTLEMEN	THE LADIES
GROOM: Prepares wedding vows, dresses up, and acts nervous all the way up to the big day.	**BRIDE:** Finds a wedding gown, acts like a crazy bitch, and avoids temptation from Jealous Ex-Boyfriend.
BEST MAN: Acts as the social planner for the whole weekend.	**MAID OF HONOR:** Coordinates the bachelorette party and works with the best man to plan day-drinking activities.
GROOMSMEN (THREE TO FOUR): Generally maintain a solid standard of intoxication throughout the weekend.	**BRIDESMAIDS (THREE TO FOUR):** Find matching ugly dresses and look bitter.
FATHER OF THE BRIDE: Constantly harasses the groom for stealing your daughter and brings cigars for everyone.	**MOTHER OF THE GROOM:** Helps the bride get ready; coordinate outfits with the father of the bride.
FATHER OF THE GROOM: Comes sharply dressed, fresh from the divorce of his fourth marriage and ready to attack the bridesmaids.	**MOTHER OF THE GROOM:** Still good-looking but recently divorced, she's the life of the party, trying to make her ex jealous.
PRIEST: Rocks a priest collar all weekend; slurs with an Irish brogue, frequently taking pulls from a flask of gin.	**DESPERATE GOLD DIGGER:** Dresses really slutty and is the one who's scheming to catch the bouquet during the toss.
WEDDING SINGER: Comes up with a name like Johnny Galaxy, and leads group dances like the Electric Slide.	**WEDDING PLANNER:** Is in charge of making sure everyone is sober enough for the actual wedding; leads the decorating of the "chapel" and banquet area.
JEALOUS EX-BOYFRIEND: Tries to seduce the bride all weekend; wears an old high school varsity jacket.	**JEALOUS EX-GIRLFRIEND:** Plays the seductress in an attempt to win back the groom.
DRUNK UNCLE: Is obnoxiously drunk during the whole reception, and consistently brings up how horrible his life's been since he blew out his knee against Miramonte High in '78.	**DRUNK AUNT:** Like her counterpart, she has to be excessively drunk at inappropriate times and often stages loud fights with her husband.

OVER THE TOP

If you really want to go the extra mile, find a house to rent for the weekend. This will act as your sleeping quarters, your ceremony area, and of course, your reception hall. Look for something with an outdoor area where you can have the ceremony. (Note: Upon arrival, take all fragile and expensive looking crap and hide it in the master bedroom closet. This will save you from losing the security deposit. Trust us.)

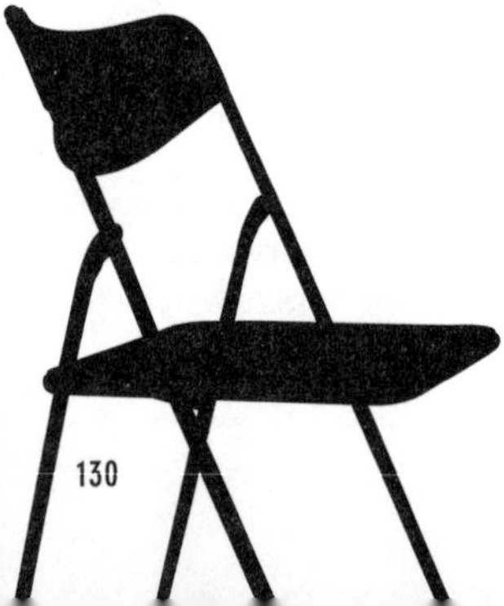

PLAYLIST

"Chapel of Love"
The Dixie Cups *(Post-Wedding Procession Song)*

"You're Nobody 'Til Somebody Loves You"
Dean Martin

"Money (That's What I Want)"
Barrett Strong *(Bouquet Toss)*

"That's Amore"
Dean Martin *(Wedding Dinner Sing-Along Song)*

"Let's Get it On"
Marvin Gaye *(Bride and Groom)*

"At Last"
Etta James *(Father/Daughter Dance)*

"Like a Prayer"
Madonna *(Bride and Bridesmaid Dance Song)*

"I'm Too Sexy"
Right Said Fred *(bring the debauchery back with the groom and his groomsmen dancing to this song)*

"We Are Family"
Sister Sledge *(cheesy but classic)*

"Mony Mony"
Billy Idol

"You Spin Me Round (Like a Record)"
Dead or Alive

"Cha Cha Slide"
Mr. C *(make the whole party do this song)*

"Bust a Move"
Young MC

NEON OR NOTHING, A.K.A. THE TIGHT AND BRIGHT PARTY

Imagine thirty friends showing up to a parking lot at 8 A.M. ready to get weird. Now imagine that everyone is decked out in the brightest neon clothes they could find at secondhand stores. There are running outfits from 1988, neon green wrestling singlets, and Madonna dresses spray painted bright pink. And here's the kicker: You're all about to get on school bus stocked with booze and then float down a river.

THE SET-UP

Synch up a playlist of Journey and REO Speedwagon to your imagined scene. Boozing, singing, dancing, and falling all over a school bus will most likely ensue. Unload and get everyone onto rafts or in inner tubes. Begin your three to four hour float down the river. Along the way, the following will probably occur:

Someone will pull someone else off the raft in a shallow area, which will result in a skinned knee.
Solution: Drink another beer.

Someone will begin a singalong to "You've Lost that Loving Feeling."
Solution: Drink another beer and join in on the chorus.

Someone will lean your head back and pour a bag of wine your throat.
Solution: Open your mouth and taste that sweet sunset blush Franzia.

A family that planned a nice quiet floating of the river for Grandma's 70th birthday will look at you with disgust, bewilderment, and a little bit of fear.
Solution: Have a girl flash the family and offer the twelve-year-old son a beer bong. America! Fuck ya!

Someone will probably say the following phrases: "forge the river," "stroke hard on the starboard-port," "man overboard," "beer overboard," "bag of wine overboard," or "commandeer their raft and steal their booze."
Solution: Do whatever your captain tells you, even if it means convincing a boat of Asian tourists to have a beer bong competition.

Now you have all been on the river for about three hours and you can see the end is near. You are wasted, sunburned, and ready to get back on the bus. You may have a few scratches on your body and you will most definitely reek of beer and river water. However, you will all get on that bus knowing that you just had a small taste of paradise.

Wizard Staffs

Every river has a beer island. It's a magical oasis where travelers can dock their rides and take the Natty-Light intake from junior varsity to Hall of Fame status. Wizard Staffs is the perfect game for your Neon or Nothing Beer Island stopover.

On the enchanted banks of Neon Island, there lives a wizard who can cast spells like the world has never seen. Actually, by "enchanted banks" we mean the muddy shores of Beer Island, by "wizard" we mean alcoholic, and by "cast spells" we mean throw up on himself.

"How can I visit this wizard?" you ask. Well, it is quite simple. Master the truly noble game of Wizard Staffs. To play, all you need are multiple thirty-packs of each wizard's favorite canned beer. And the magical epoxy that has been passed down for ages—*duct tape*. Then let the games begin!

Assemble all of the competing wizards on Beer Island and finish your first canned beer. Congratulations honorable sir, you are now a *level one* wizard. "But how do I change levels and improve my spells?" Simple. Put a full beer on top of the recently finished one and tape them together with the duct tape. Once that beer is finished you will be a *level two* wizard. Continue gaining magical prowess by adding beers to your staff and finishing them off.

Wizards will begin to notice that the longer their staffs become, the more powers they seem to have. These powers include invulnerability to insults, the ability to time travel into the future (blackout), and at *level sixteen*, the ability to piss oneself.

But be careful. As you and your fellow wizards become more powerful, it will become apparent that only one can rule Beer Island. Once you've reached *level eight*, the battling can begin. Use your staffs as weapons and fight to the death . . . or until someone breaks his staff. The one with the longest staff at day's end will rule the Island. Godspeed, young magician.

PLAYLIST

Obnoxious singalong songs:

"Blue Monday"
New Order

"Whip It"
Devo

"Your Love"
The Outfield

"I Want Candy"
Bow Wow Wow

"Tainted Love"
Soft Cell

"867-5309/Jenny"
Tommy Tutone

"We're Not Gonna to Take It"
Twisted Sister

"Funkytown"
Lipps, Inc.

"Hot Hot Hot"
Buster Poindexter

"Down Under"
Men at Work

"Lean on Me"
Club Nouveau

"Two of Hearts"
Stacey Q

"Genius of Love"
Tom Tom Club

"I'm So Excited"
The Pointer Sisters

NINTENDO OLYMPICS

Hey nerd! It's time to finally put all those wasted hours during your childhood to use. People may have mocked you in the past for skipping the sock hop to beat the *Legend of Zelda* and they probably still mock you now. At least they will be making fun of a Nintendo Olympic champion. Gather some gamer friends and see whose thumbs rule the galaxy of Mom's basement.

THE SET-UP

Invite eight friends over to compete for the Fred "Wizard" Savage Trophy. Go to a *www.PrintyourBrackets.com* and set up an eight-man, double elimination bracket. Pick a combination of classic NES games, Super NES, and Wii games.

With the Wii, you can purchase old Nintendo games if you have an Internet connection. Organize a Nintendo Olympics that combines the new Wii sports games and old classics like *Tecmo Bowl*, *Ice Hockey*, *Mario Tennis*, and *Bases Loaded*. The best part is that you turn the Wii controller's sideways and use it just like the classic NES controller.

Embrace Your Inner Nerd

Here are five tips on how to let out the geek inside.

1. Pick an obscure Nintendo character as your contestant name: You could go with Don Flamenco, King Hippo, or Soda Popinski (*Punch-Out!!*), Rash, Zitz, or Pimple (*Battletoads*), Simon Belmont (*Castlevania*), Red Falcon (the evil alien organization in *Contra*), Solid Snake (*Metal Gear*), or Bubble Bobble, Kid Icarus, or Diddy Kong who all had their own games.

2. Spend $30 at 7-Eleven on a nerd cornucopia of sugary snacks: Mountain Dew: Code Red, Ho-Hos, Twinkies, Sour Patch Kids, Red Bulls, and Sour Skittles. Feel that? It's your eyes popping out of your head like a pug on meth and your muffin tops spilling over the elastic in your sweat pants. Can you play through the pain?

3. Spaz out for Domino's pizza: Give each player a pen and a piece of paper. Everyone gets one minute to list as many NES video games as they can. The two people with the least amount of names have to buy the pizza.

4. Make it known to the virtual world: The first person eliminated from the tournament has to set their Facebook status as "Hey ladies, I just recently purchased the box set of *Planet of the Apes* and was wondering if any of you would like to come over for some Mountain Dew, a foot massage, and a movie marathon? Let me know."

5. Turn on your own kind: The runner-up to the competition has to call a local comic book store and impersonate Ogre by screaming, "Nerds! I *hate* Nerds!" This must continue until they hang up.

ONE PERSON'S TRASH IS ANOTHER PERSON'S TREASURE PARTY

Sometimes drinking twelve shots of Jägermeister and making out next to a dumpster isn't the best way to start a relationship. Instead, you should focus on the lost art of conversation. But with whom? In your twenties, the best people to meet and strike up a conversation with are friends of friends. Therefore the 5th Year is going to keep it (somewhat) classy and show you how to get everyone in your party talking. And maybe, if things go right, making out next to a dumpster after twelve shots of Jäger.

THE SET-UP

For the One Person's Trash Is Another Person's Treasure Party, each attendee must bring one platonic friend of the opposite sex. Think of this party as speed dating meets a swap meet. Your platonic friend can either be an ex, coworker, or family member, just make sure it's not your significant other. Anyone you bring to this party is open game.

Dance Away the Awkward

You're about to have a houseful of people who don't really know each other. Music and alcohol are always the best icebreakers. This is a simple way to ease the awkwardness of the party. Buy a greatest hits album from a famous band, take a group shot every time the track changes, and see where the night goes.

***Turn It On Again: The Hits*—Genesis:** Nothing screams 1980s manic-depressive coke bender better than Genesis. If your friends aren't rocking out by track number five, "I Can't Dance," then you might as well pull a Zach Braff and pound a bottle of Nyquil while watching *Garden State.*

***The Very Best of Prince*—Prince:** Why do men have nipples? What is the purpose of life? How can men so pretty still ooze heterosexuality? Prince's greatest hits will answer all that remains unanswered. Do group karaoke to "Purple Rain" and bring back the up-tempo dance party with track number nine, "Kiss."

***Greatest Hits*—Devo:** Most people only know their big hit "Whip It," but these Ohio born synthpunk pioneers have a slew of rocking party songs. The band's signature was the red plastic hats. Guess what? They're only $15 online. Order some before your party.

***The Best of Blondie*—Blondie:** Debbie Harry worked at a Dunkin Donuts before recording six amazing albums under the moniker Blondie. So don't give up on your heavy metal band, Goblincock. There is still hope. But in the meantime, buy this disco and reggae infused new wave album and give out rum-based shooter concoctions during "The Tide is High."

***Loud, Fast Ramones: Their Toughest Hits*—The Ramones:** This album will magically transport you from your Crate and Barrel flat to your parent's basement while they're out at a movie for two hours! By the first song, you and your friends will be crushing Pabst Blue Ribbons like juice-boxes and wanting to finger bang each other in the closet—just like in high school. This album will make you want to drink with a reckless abandon. Jack Daniels shots required; mainlining speed with urinal water is not.

Tip: Play your choice *Greatest Hits* then hit the bars like a group that's been together forever.

OUTDOOR CONCERT

"Dude, we need to find some 'shrooms, the Stones are playing in Billy's backyard."

Everyone's way too dead. All of the great rock starts have either choked on their own vomit, or have been institutionalized for various addictive qualities. Our generation has a fleet of tight-legged Emos who wouldn't know rock and roll if it bit them in their iced-latte-holding mitten fingers. The only revolution we're going to experience is the green revolution, which is cool, but doesn't really involve music, sex, or drugs. That's mostly just Al Gore speeches and making sure you put your shit in the right recycling bin. So for old time's sake, and the sake of really good live rock, throw an Outdoor Concert, with a seriously killer lineup.

THE SET-UP

A venue where you can blast music is important. Try finding a place on someone's private property so you won't be bothered by Johnny Law or Phil McAngry-Neighbor. Open field areas, rooftops, or big backyards are ideal. Just make sure there are power outlets so that you don't have to rent a generator.

Take it from the 5th Year:

- *Beg, borrow, or steal audio visual equipment. Worst case scenario is to rent from a video rental warehouse. If you have a small budget, check out the inflatable movie screens at www.funflicks.com.*
- *Fill buckets with alcohol and ice or buy kegs.*
- *Show the concert DVDs at night for lighting purposes.*

ROCK STAR PARTY GAME: BROWNIE ROULETTE

We're not suggesting you vomit an eighth of mushrooms on the wall and then stare at the trippy hallucinations like Jerry Garcia did. And we're not suggesting that you take sixty valiums in one day like Elton John. Nor are we asking you to swallow so many drugs at the Japanese Customs Office that you go into a ninety-six hour coma like the guitarist from Guns N' Roses. No, we're not recommending anything like that. All we're saying to do is to make two tins of brownies:

- One should be dark chocolate, and one should be special.
- Cut them into individual squares, wrap them in napkins, and place them on a counter-top.
- Before you start the concert DVD, have everyone pick a brownie and eat it quickly.
- A half-hour into the show, look into the crowd and you will easily be able to pick out who scored the dark chocolate.

5TH YEAR'S FAVORITE CONCERT DVDS

Led Zeppelin:
Led Zeppelin

U2:
Elevation Tour 2001

The Rolling Stones:
Four Flicks

Paul McCartney:
Live at the Cavern Club

Bruce Springsteen and the E Street Band:
Live in New York

Pink Floyd:
Live at Pompeii

The Who:
Live at Royal Albert Hall

Talking Heads:
Stop Making Sense

Kings of Leon:
Live at the O2 (London)

Bob Marley:
Live in Concert (Germany)

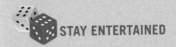

STAY ENTERTAINED

What's an outdoor concert without some Frisbee? Set up a game of Beersbee, which requires two posts forty feet apart. Place two beer cans atop each post. Take turns throwing a Frisbee to try and knock the cans off the post. Official rules, scoring, and Beersbee sets can be found on their website, *www.beersbee.org*.

PIZZA COOK-OFF

You got your dough, you got your sauce, you got your cheese, you got your more cheese, and you got your green stuff. Think you're ready to make a pie? I guess we'll have to settle the time-honored pizza debate in the kitchen. The Pizza Cook-Off is different from your average Friday night of getting sloppy drunk and making out with a forty-year-old schoolteacher. Instead, invite some friends over for an Iron Chef Pizza Cook-Off.

THE SET-UP

The Cook-Off aims to find the most creative and tastiest pizza possible. Every person is responsible for his or her own pizza during the cook-off. Alliances will be formed and sabotaging may occur, so protect your pizza at all times. Making a mess is an entertaining part of the process. Do not be afraid to get your hands and your clothes dirty. Send threatening e-mails prior to the event, just to let people know that you are one step away from Papa John himself. This will breed a competitive spirit during the cook-off. Look up recipes, ask your grandmother, call Domino's, do whatever you have to do to win.

Trader Joe's is a great spot for ingredients. Most stores will have fresh dough separated into bags, cheeses, meats, sauces, vegetables, and other surprise toppings. Have everyone cast their ballots for best pizza into a hat. Let everyone know who the winner is, and prepare to feast down on some homemade pie.

AFTER THE PIZZA PARTY, BREAK OUT THE CARDS. THE FIRST TWO PEOPLE TO LOSE ALL THEIR CHIPS HAVE TO DO ALL THE DISHES. THE WINNERS FINISH THE GAME WHILE VERBALLY ASSAULTING THE LABORERS IN THE KITCHEN. START WITH A SMALL AMOUNT OF CHIPS AND HAVE MANDATORY ANTES ON EVERY HAND. THIS FORCES AGGRESSIVE PLAY AND PREVENTS ASSHOLES FROM FOLDING EVERY GAME.

Ten Truly Italian Pies

- *Rudy's BBQ Gulianni:* chicken, prosciutto, BBQ sauce, diced onion, mozzarella, jalapeño, gouda cheese, cilantro
- *The Joey Tribianni Tribute to Sausage:* Italian sausage, mozzarella, garlic, olive oil, salt, no sauce
- *The Pesto Fonzarelli:* fresh pesto, ricotta cheese, fresh tomato diced, mozzarella, garlic, pine nuts
- *The DeVito Deepdish with Sausage and Shrimp:* extra sausage and shrimp, mozzarella, garlic, sauce, fresh tomatoes
- *The Rocky Bal-Bacon:* bacon diced mixed in ricotta cheese, diced tomatoes, garlic, sauce
- *The Greasy Little Italian:* pepperoni, sausage, mushrooms, mozzarella, sauce (Joe Pesci's favorite)
- *The Marco con Pollo:* chicken, tomato, garlic, onions, mozzarella, sauce
- *Franco's Sardinian Strongman with Sardines:* Parmesan cheese, mozzarella cheese, provolone cheese, Romano cheese, sardines, tuna, thin crust, and egg whites, no sauce
- *The Joe Montana Meatball:* meatballs cut in half, sauces, mozzarella, garlic
- *The Prosciutto DiMaggio:* tons of prosciutto, tons of Swiss cheese, garlic, sauce

TND! THURSDAY NIGHT DINNER

The Thursday Night Dinner is a trustworthy event that can help build your social network. It's hard to maintain a dinner every week, so have two or three a month. This is a great way to bring new people into your group by inviting them over for a themed dinner party. Meeting good people at bars is never a guarantee. The TND is a way to control your environment by inviting the right people. Building trust through these casual dinners can create a long-lasting party crew for the bigger theme party events. Here are ten creative dinner party ideas:

1. Mahi Mahi Tacos and Mojitos
2. Rolling Rocks and Ribs
3. Tiger Shrimp Kabobs and Tsing Taos
4. Mustard and Margaritas (buy a variety of sausage meat and gourmet mustards to dip)
5. Lobstertails and Lowenbrau
6. Fishsticks and Fosters
7. Corn Flake French Toast and Champagne (like breakfast for dinner)
8. Smoked Meat and Smokey Scotch
9. Equis and Enchilidas (make sure to drink more than *dos*)
10. Tapas and Two-Buck Chuck
11. Grilled Cheese and Grenades (Mickey's Grenades, of course)

THURSDAY NIGHT DINNER PARTY FAVORS

Aside from alcohol, Victorian masks are the single greatest party icebreaker of all time. Let people get a few cocktails down before you unveil these gems. Then sit back and watch hilarity ensue. When people put these masks on their faces transform and they will adopt a whole new persona. Your sides will hurt from laughing so hard. Make sure you take plenty of pictures. Order some today. Look for them on *www.wowcoolstuff.com.*

PROM IN YOUR PRIME

Hmmm . . . sober dancing, a ticking virginity clock, and premature ejaculation. Let's revisit that moment shall we? It's time to spring a move on your date, Mary Jane Rottencrotch. You know she's easy, at least that's what it says on the bathroom stall. You go in for the kiss, and blammo! Your uncontrollable boner pokes her before you can tuck it into your Mervyn's belt. She laughs and points at the chub tenting your Dockers. Mary Jane tells everyone and you get stuck with the nickname, "Boner Jam." High school is ruined . . . until now.

THE SET-UP

Ever wanted a chance to relive the night of the "boner coaster?" It's easy. Throw your prom night number two. This time around, you will hopefully be able to control your vascular issues. Replace acne and chaperones with an open bar and whiskey dick. You're in your prime. So act like it. The only thing missing the first time around was control of the photo booth and hundreds of dollars worth of cheap champagne. Just like your first prom, taking the date picture is the big moment of the night. Smile, look good, and make sure to tuck in your gullet. The same rules apply this time around. Set up a photo area with a backdrop. People love getting in front of the camera for the big shot. The only difference is that you will undoubtedly be eight or nine beers into the night. There aren't any teachers to tell you to behave. Feel free to do whatever you want and let your wildest prom photo dreams come true.

The Rules

- *Force all guests to bring a date and to dress up in theme.*
- *Set up a picture booth. This can be a digital camera with a cloth backdrop, a sign, and some stars, etc.*
- *If you don't have an eye for style, ask your girlfriends to help with decorations. Party America is cheapest place to find prom decorations.*
- *Free reign in pictures. Mangyna the shit out of those pics!*
- *Hire a security guard to take money at the door and to keep the peace.*
- *Scrap bartenders, let people go at the alcohol for a flat fee: $35 or $45.*
- *DJs are easier than live music.*
- *Only serve clear alcohol, for obvious security deposit reasons.*
- *Have a male and female dance-off to award Homecoming King and Queen.*

Glory Days

5th Year has been the epicenter of mischief since we attended a Catholic high school together. Here's a countdown of our top ten most memorable moments from back in the day (excluding some of the ones that could still involve prosecution).

10. The first time we drank, we paid a bearded Harley dude to buy the booze, drank two forties of Mickey's, and vomited on a lawn for three hours.

9. This one time we rolled down a steep hill laughing hysterically (like in *Princess Bride*) with thirty friends and a keg because the cops raided our party.

8. Our friend, Critter, was so drunk at the school fashion show that he fell off the stage and directly onto the table of the school president.

7. Our friend, Matt, stapled his cheat sheet to his test and turned it in. Mr. Breen didn't report him but tortured him all year.

6. We sold a huge bag of oregano to freshmen then watched them smoke it and pretend to be high off marijuana. We used the money to buy beer.

5. We bought over $200 worth of bouncy balls and distributed them to every male in our class. Then our friend Tony snuck into the main office and put on Guns and Roses' "Welcome to the Jungle" over the school P.A. This triggered a bouncy ball war that made the gym look like a giant particle reactor.

4. Dominic got arrested at sixteen years old while trying to buy beer at Safeway with a Montana fake ID under the alias, Buck Reed.

3. We ran for Publicity Office under the slogan "Con+Dom! It's a safe bet!"

2. On St. Patrick's Day, we paraded a keg of root beer into the courtyard of our high school and proceeded to organize boat races with freshmen kids.

1. The fact that we filmed every party during high school and know that we can retire off the shoebox full of blackmail because our friends are becoming lawyers, doctors, and cops.

PLAYLIST

Nostalgic high school songs, fun must-plays, and a few slow dances:

"Smooth"
Rob Thomas & Santana (*reminds me of every prom*)

"Beware of the Boys"
Panjabi MC (*my friends are weird but there is nothing better than a bunch of people rocking out to this song*)

"Tennessee"
Arrested Development

"Slam"
Onyx

"Jump Around"
House of Pain (*song for guys who couldn't dance*)

"Humpty Dance"
Digital Underground

"Hip Hop Hooray"
Naughty by Nature

"Two Princes"
Spin Doctors

"Rump Shaker"
Wreckx-N-Effect

"Mambo No. 5"
Lou Bega

"Jump"
Kriss Kross

"Informer"
Snow

"Your Woman"
White Town

"I Got a Man"
Positive K

"Ditty"
Paperboy

"Blue (Da Ba Dee)"
Eiffel 65

"Time After Time"
Cyndi Lauper

"All Out of Love"
Air Supply

"Lady in Red"
Chris de Burgh

"November Rain"
Guns N' Roses

RAT PACK PARTY

"I feel sorry for people who don't drink. They wake up in the morning and that's the best they're going to feel all day."

—Frank Sinatra

The Rat Pack was made up of Frank Sinatra, Dean Martin, Sammy Davis Jr., and Joey Bishop. These guys were simply badass. And it'd be an honor for you to even pretend to be them for one night. So do your best.

THE SET-UP

Throwing a Rat Pack party is paying tribute to benders in Vegas, smart cocktails, and smoking cigars. These were the originals that made drinking cool. This cirrhosis super-group will always symbolize 1960s Las Vegas style. When you're decorating your place, think big-band glamour. You can use Google's image search to find pictures of the Pack and get ideas for costumes.

OVER THE TOP

Rent a lounge with '60s decor to give the party an old-school Vegas feel. The most important part of a Rat Pack Party is obviously the booze. You really only have one of two options when it comes to what should be served at this event—the Manhattan or the martini.

The Manhattan is a cocktail made with whiskey, sweet vermouth, and bitters. Commonly used whiskeys include rye (the traditional choice), Canadian, bourbon, and Tennessee. Proportions of whiskey to vermouth vary, from a very sweet one to one ratio to a much less sweet four to one ratio. That means four pouring seconds of alcohol, to one pouring second of vermouth, using a pour spout of course. The cocktail is often stirred with ice and strained into a cocktail glass, where it is garnished with a Maraschino cherry with a stem. Done.

The martini is a cocktail made with gin and dry white vermouth, substituting vodka for gin is popular as well. Simply pour the alcohol (vodka or gin) and the dry vermouth over ice and shake. The proportions should be four to one, alcohol to vermouth. Shake contents, and pour into a cocktail glass. Garnish with two olives on a toothpick. Finito.

DRESS THE PART

Guys: Striped suits, thin ties, greased hair, flat tops, tennis club sweaters, checkered pants, fedora hats, cigars, fake cash stacks, velour shirts or sweaters, and white shoes.

Girls: Polka dot dresses, pulled-back hair, red lipstick, red fingernails, stiletto heels, pearl necklaces, curled hairdos or bouffants, cigarette holders, and dark pantyhose.

RED WINE/WHITE SUIT PARTY

Did you know red wine takes out white wine stains; red wine is good for your heart; and keeping your white clothes clean at the Red Wine/White Suit Party is very plausible? Some of those may or may not be true, it's up to you to find out. This party is special, and should be reserved for special occasions, you know, like Saturdays. This event has a very self-explanatory title . . . that mixes red wine with expendable white clothing to form one amazing night of spills, thrills, and purple teeth.

THE SET-UP

This party should be thrown outdoors. Don't use your mother's house with the shag carpets. If you do (you have been forewarned), send us the pictures; I'm sure it will look awesome. Pick an indestructible area or a place with a nice big grassy area that is easy to clean up. You will be making a mess here, so focus on the party, and not how much shit you are ruining.

Once you have your destination set, make the invite. Let everyone know that it is a Red Wine/White Suit Party. You don't want someone showing up in their grandma's white wedding gown, only to find themselves covered in two-buck Chuck. Don't wear nice clothes, but make sure they are white. Anyone who shows up to the party without full white clothing on will be booed and asked to leave. Rules are rules. On their way out, spray them with the red wine hose.

Try one of these competitions or check out the wine games listed in the Tour de Franzia.

- *Long distance wine spit*
- *Best wine spit smiley face on someone's back*
- *Best red wine teeth award (whitest teeth = Least Valuable Player)*
- *Anchorman with a pitcher of wine*
- *Wine hose in da nose—snort it!*
- *Avoid getting spilled on the longest game*

The next morning get twenty friends to go to IHOP in their red stained clothes and enjoy some delicious boysenberry pancakes while elderly citizens stare at you in disgust. Like we said, "If you can't fuck them . . . take a joke!"

OVER THE TOP

If you want to get really adventurous, combine this party with Day at the Track . . . rent a private group area at a track and let the games begin. (We did this and it rocked—we were booted after three hours.)

SEVEN PARTIES P. DIDDY SHOULD BE THROWING, A.K.A. OFFENSIVE AND EXPENSIVE PARTY IDEAS

If financial constraints were not an issue and you were known for throwing great parties, don't you think you could come up with something more creative than a "white party"? Well, you can't expect too much from a rapper who uses the same alias that kindergartners use to describe their genitals. Here is a list of seven horribly offensive and expensive parties that Diddy should be throwing:

1. Exotic Bird/BB Gun Party

That's right Method Man. Go down to your local zoo, buy a yellow cockatoo, and protect that endangered species with yo life, son. The last person whose endangered bird is alive gets the controlling stake of the Charlotte Bobcats. "Quick! Chamillionaires's toucan is having a seizure, keep shooting!"

2. Day Laborer Gladiator Fights

Ever seen a gold-toothed Guatemalan lean out of an '87 Datsun and hit a Nicaraguan with a trident? Pull out your Roman throwback jerseys (togas) for this wine-soaked bloodbath and then cheer on your favorite gladiator, Mexamus Aurelius, while scantily-clad Brazilian models feed you grapes.

3. Mormon Handcuff Party

Fly a private jet to Salt Lake City. Tell a bunch of Mormons there are free Hasbro board games inside and then fly them to Vegas. Everyone at the party gets handcuffed to one Mormon of the same sex. Whoever can convince their Mormon to commit the worst sin wins a Ferrari.

4. Cristal Piss Party

Don't confuse this with the R. Kelly party where everyone actually pees on each other. The Cristal Piss Party is simple. Separate into co-ed teams of four. Each team gets a case of Cristal champagne and one champagne bucket. First team to properly fill their champagne bucket with Cristal urine wins a lifetime supply of Proactiv Acne Solution.

5. Robo Jocks Party

Rent a large open field. Every partygoer gets a scissor lift on wheels, a refrigerated Jägermeister machine, and a paintball gun. Instructions and/or rules are subject to change.

6. Never-Ending New Year's Eve 747 High Stakes Casino Party

Design a double-decker 747 jumbo jet with a casino. Start at the Greenwich Meridian timeline in London and take off at December 31st at 9 P.M. A nonstop flight from London to Honolulu takes fourteen hours and takes you back ten time zones. Along the way celebrate New Year's in Chicago and Los Angeles then arrive in Honolulu early on New Year's Eve for the biggest bash.

7. San Francisco's Running of the Homeless

Prior to the event, partygoers will be shipped gowns or tuxedos covered in $5 bills. Like Spain's running of the bulls, the party will start in the narrow streets of downtown San Francisco. Homeless participants will be given methamphetamines before the chase. Once the homeless zombies are released, partygoers have to run to the country club across town. Once inside the safe haven, there will be a champagne toast and a tally to see which partygoer still has the most money. The winner receives a free maid for a year so he/she can volunteer at the day care center where the maid puts her kids.

ROMANCE NOVEL PARTY

Has Valentine's Day become a monotonous custom? While your snobby waiter rambles about the flavors in your Chilean wine do you wonder if other couples are having amazing Diane Lane and French dude sex? Well, they're not. They are having the same boring conversation at another overpriced restaurant. Shouldn't this holiday be a celebration? A badge of honor that tells everyone, "I've been with this guy for three years and I haven't stabbed him in the neck yet?"

When it comes to V-day, guys severely lack creativity; even a John Cusack movie marathon wouldn't spark a romantic idea. Girls, it's time you take control. Fire up a few of your girlfriends and throw a Romance Novel Party.

THE SET-UP

Take your partner to a used bookstore and search for the tackiest, tasteless, yet somewhat erotic romance novel cover. Take the time to find the perfect trifecta:

1. Good cover art costumes (guys should be ready to be shirtless and sporting a Fabio wig)
2. Imaginative pose with male and female characters
3. A great title (examples: *Undead and Unwed*, *Snowdrops and Scandalbroth*, *The Return of Rafe Mackade*, *Deidre and Don Juan*, *The Bride Wore Spurs*, *Caress and Conquer*, and *The Sweet Savage Love*)

Then, go to a vintage clothing store and find the exact replicas of your chosen cover art costumes. Remember, this is a competition and victory is won with attention to details. While you're out, pick up some things to help set the mood. Decorations should include lots of scented candles. (Girls, you know how to set the mood better than we do.)

In the invitation to the party, make it clear that every couple should bring at least two bottles of wine and a dish to share. The food should be light, simple, and sensual. The end goal is to go home and make passionate love—not to fill up on chicken wings and play Dutch oven.

Food Suggestions

- *Fondue*
- *Tomato and mozzarella salad*
- *Shrimp cocktail*
- *Cheese and fruit plate*
- *Chocolate covered strawberries*

Use a dark bed sheet to create a photo backdrop. Before dinner (but after a few glasses of vino) make all the couples recreate their romance novel pose in front of the backdrop. And if your friends are really creative (and/or drunk enough), make them perform a short passage from their book. Before the night's over, send a bowl around the table and have partygoers vote for their favorite costume. Votes should be based on which couple created the closest replica.

BREAK OUT THE "HELLO MY NAME IS" STICKERS AND MAKE EVERYONE WRITE DOWN THE NAMES OF THEIR ROMANCE NOVEL CHARACTERS.

STAY ENTERTAINED

Once everyone is full but not too full, launch into some Movie Trivia: Infamous Sex Scenes and Romantic Comedy Edition. Here are a few sample questions (a full quiz can be found on *www.5thYear.com*):

Which actor also in the movie *Top Gun* was offered the lead role in *Dirty Dancing* but declined?

Val Kilmer

In what 2006 film is a woman seen fully nude in an airplane lavatory having sexual intercourse with a man, right before getting bitten on the nipple by a snake?

Snakes on a Plane

What song does Rupert Everett get the family to start singing at the restaurant scene in *My Best Friend's Wedding*?

Aretha Franklin's "I Say a Little Prayer for You"

PLAYLIST

This is more romantic than Javier Bardem ripping off Kiera Knightley's duchess dress while a castle burns down on the beach during a peasant revolution under a full moon.

"Sympathique"
Pink Martini

"Feeling Good"
Nina Simone (Trouble Maker remix)

"Let's Never Stop Falling in Love"
Pink Martini

"Samba Pa Ti"
Santana

"Lunatico"
Gotan Project

"Mas Que Nada"
Sergio Mendes and the Brazil '66

"Diablo Rojo"
Rodrigo Y Gabriela

"Tamacun"
Rodrigo Y Gabriela

"Non, Je Ne Regrette Rien"
Edith Piaf

"Love Me, Please Love Me"
Michel Polnareff

"Bolero"
Pink Martini

"Chan Chan"
Buena Vista Social Club

"Bamboleo"
Gipsy Kings

"Suavamente"
Elvis Crespo

"Oh Marie"
Louis Prima

"Clandestino"
Manu Chao

"I Can't Help Falling in Love With You"
UB40

"Just a Gigolo"
Louis Prima

"At Last"
Etta James

"In the Air Tonight"
Phil Collins (*close the party with the lights off and a pitch black sing-along*)

RO-SHAM-BO TOURNAMENT

Cram sixty-four competitors (drunk friends) into one arena (dive bar) to compete in one big Ro-Sham-Bo Tournament (shitshow). Contrary to popular belief, the Egyptians invented Ro-Sham-Bo. Those smart pharaohs also invented beer and that's pretty much all you need for this event. Unless you've recently been caught stealing in Saudi Arabia, then you might have to sit this one out—because they chop off your hands.

THE SET-UP

Use butcher paper to post large March Madness style competition brackets on the wall. Set up three tables and have three games running at a time.

Drunk people can become difficult to wrangle. Make sure you designate a master of ceremonies and three referees to keep the matches moving quickly.

Bring wigs, glasses, bandanas, and fake noses for different themed rounds. This is a perfect event for a fundraiser because you can charge an entrance fee and give contestants branded t-shirts.

BEAR, NINJA, COWBOY

BNC is Ro-Sham-Bo but with body poses instead of hand signs. So if you want to change things up for your tourney, you can always go Bear, Ninja, Cowboy instead of Rock, Paper, Scissors. Stand back to back with your opponent. On a three count, you must turn and face each other in one of the poses.

Bear: Hands above head in a claw formation. Scary growling encouraged.

Ninja: Hands crossed at chest level like you are about to karate fight.

Cowboy: Both index fingers pointed like six shooters at hip level.

What beats what:
Bear mauls Ninja

Ninja karate chops Cowboy

Cowboy shoots Bear

The Rules

All matches are best two out of three until the Final Four, which is five out of seven. Each referee holds a stack of note cards with a losing punishment. Prior to the match, each contestant would pick a note card and if they lost, they had to do whatever was on the card. These cards add extra incentive for the contestants.

Loser Bets

- Top Gun *high five the bartender*
- *Awkward prom pose with the winner*
- *Winner gives loser a noogie*
- *Cell Phone Roulette: Scroll through contracts when winner says "stop" call that person and yell "Ro-Sham-Bo motherfucker!"*
- *Armpit fart*
- *Worm dance*
- *Buy a beer for winner*
- *Buy a shot for winner*
- *Propose to referee of your choice*
- *Winner gets to perform favorite WWE move to loser*
- *Take a bar mat shot*
- *Shake face into camera*
- *Flubber winner's stomach (blow onto skin making fart noise)*
- *Winner gives loser a wet willie*

ROYAL RUMBLE PARTY

"Oooooh yeah!!! *What you gonna do brotha when Hulkamania runs wild on you? I tell you what you're gonna do brotha, bet on the Royal Rumble, brotha. Thirty men enter, but only one can be champion. To all my little Hulkamaniacs, say your prayers, eat your vitamins, and let's get ready to rumble!"*

Every January the WWE has an event called the Royal Rumble. It starts with two wrestlers in the ring. Every two minutes, there is a countdown and another wrestler enters. It goes all the way up to thirty wrestlers. Contestants can only be eliminated by getting thrown over the top rope.

THE SET-UP

We have devised a system of gambling on the event that you can do with your friends.

Here's the rundown:

1. Order the WWE's *Royal Rumble* on pay-per-view or buy an old DVD version if you're a cheap-o.
2. Organize fifteen people and have everyone throw $10 into a pot.
3. Fill one hat with numbers one to fifteen.
4. Fill another hat with numbers sixteen to thirty.
5. Each player gets to select one number from each hat. Each number has an unknown wrestler attached. Whatever two numbers you select become your wrestlers. Trading is strictly prohibited. The contestant who has the number of the last wrestler in the ring wins the pot of money.

In true *Royal Rumble* fashion, the countdown for each new wrestler spurs some chanting. Whoever has the next number will speak up and start the shit talking. There is nothing better than having him get the "no name wrestler" in the red Speedo. This starts more shit talking because the "no-names" are sure to get tossed out immediately. The Rumbles always end with a dramatic twist, so be ready for a controversial finale.

We started by ordering these on pay-per-view but it was so fun we started purchasing old *Royal Rumbles* from the early '90s with guys like Coco Beware, Hacksaw Jim Dugan, the Legion of Doom, and the Big Boss Man. These are almost better to rent (as long as no one tries to figure out who won the event beforehand).

We awarded the first place with $100, second $40 dollars, and third received their money back. We've also done one *Royal Rumble* for "winner takes all." The financial structure is up to you. Make sure you have plenty of light beer, corn dogs, Slim Jims, potato chips and mayonnaise . . . and the rest will take care of itself.

OVER THE TOP . . . ROPE IDEAS

Here are five fictitious wrestlers we would love to see in the WWE. Feel free to come dressed in one of these easily assembled costumes.

The Boston Wannabe: Decked out in a combination of '90s Sox and Celtics gear, he thinks he's badass—except he grew up on the South Shore.

Finishing Move: The Blood Mary—he strangles his opponent from behind with a rosary while his pikey cousins smash bottles on the guy's head.

The Berkley Professor: A great persona for female wrestling fans, she wears Birkenstocks and hemp clothing.

Finishing Move: The Hillary Clinton Muff Bomb—when her opponent is lying on the mat, she jumps off the top rope and delivers a double hammer-fist to the balls causing him to sit up right into her odorous muff; instant KO.

BOTDL: This very muscular seemingly tough black wrester is actually into dudes. That's right, he's a brother on the down low (BOTDL).

Finishing Move: The Erectile Dysfunctioner—he puts your Ultimate Warrior (penis) in between his butt cheeks and rips your dick off.

Mr. Bedazzle: This rhinestoned douche bag loves showing off to the crowd with his super shiny sequin underwear and boots. He's pretty lame looking, but has no idea everyone makes fun of the way he dresses. He thinks people are whispering about how much they like his sparkly bling.

Finishing Move: The Axe Body Spray Suplex—Mr. B hides a full can of Tsunami Axe Body Spray in his glittery Speedo. He sprays you in the face causing temporary blindness and follows with a fake-tan suplex.

The Poor Kid: This wrestler is so poor you can smell it, literally. He is the dirtiest, smelliest wrestler on the circuit. He defends himself by stinking opponents out of the ring. His parents were homeless window washers, so he's "made it big." He is, the Poor Kid.

Finishing Move: The Salvation Army Drop—first, he snot-rockets in your eyes, then he jumps off the top rope knocking you unconscious. When you're out cold, he takes your clothes and sells them to Salvation Army.

RUBIK'S CUBE PARTY

When Hungarian engineer Erno Rubik invented the Rubik's cube in 1974, do you think he had any idea that theme party enthusiasts would turn it into a spandex clad shit-show? That's right, dress up in preteen colors and plan to drink your face off because you're playing for your clothes—and your pride.

The Rubik's Cube Party requires everyone to wear a combination of six pieces of clothing and accessories representing every color on the Rubik's cube: green, white, blue, red, orange, and yellow. Each player is required to wear shorts and a shirt but can accessorize with hats, beanies, sunglasses, wristbands, armbands, headbands, tights, gloves, or wigs.

THE SET-UP

Depending on the amount of people at the party, the referee should split everyone into six equal teams. Then have team captains pick their color out of a hat. Each team is assigned one of the six Rubik's cube colors.

Each team has to challenge other teams to contests in order to win the right to switch one article of clothing. For example: the green team challenges the white team in a Flip Cup match. If the green team wins, each teammate gets to switch an article of clothing with the losing white team. The winning team is the first team to be dressed entirely in their own color.

The Rules

1. The referee should have two hats, one that contains the six team colors and the other that contains the drinking games. For each round, the referee draws two team colors and one challenge. Teams play one game per round.
2. A round lasts until every team has played once. If a team pulls the same challenge twice in a row, the referee is allowed to redraw. However, same team draws are allowed because it will cultivate rivalries and allow comeback.
3. The host should choose a selected number of rounds or time limit. If no team has won, the team with the most articles of their own color is deemed the winner.

STAY ENTERTAINED

Not all challenges will involve the whole team. Some games will force teams to pick the best candidate.

Team Challenges

- Flip Cup
- Boat Race
- Anchorman
- Suck and Blow
- Tallest Human Pyramid (only do once)
- Pop balloons in three different sexual positions
- You Got Served Dance Off (The opposing team picks the song; one minute per team.)
- Categories (Both teams stand in a circle; the referee picks a category—like items in a brown bag lunch, '80s movies, cartoon characters—and the person who stops or repeats something loses it for their team.)

Individual Challenges

- Best two out of three handstand competition
- Beer Bong Race
- Spelling Bee
- Rap Battle
- One-on-One Air Guitar Challenge
- Trivia

Raid a Goodwill the day before and pick up extra clothing. Just make sure everything's tight and bright. Pick three referees to regulate the event. Some of the events are subjective contests so they will have to deliberate to pick a winner.

5TH YEAR SCAVENGER HUNT

Have you ever stuffed a handful of Victoria Secret bargain panties into your mouth right after a game of leapfrog with a homeless man? If not, you need to get a group of your boldest friends together to try the 5th Year Scavenger Hunt.

THE SET-UP

1. Agree on a punishment for the losing team like Mystic Tans, or use one of our favorites and make the losers go see *A True Cinderella Story* while wearing makeup and '80s prom dresses.
2. Split into two teams and give each team a video camera.
3. Hand out the list of challenges and start the clock.
4. Each team has three hours to race around town trying to tally as many points as possible. Every

challenge must be documented on video or it does not count.

5. All items on the list are scored on a scale of one to five, five being the most difficult.
6. Each team must be back to the house by the third hour. Watch the videos. Crack some Steves. Tally your points.

Steves: Coors Light beer (because guys named Steve drink Coors Light).

The Rules

1. Every team must have one sober driver.
2. Every team must have at least one female.
3. Points can only be counted for items/activities captured on video.

The List

Use this as a starting point and add some of your own.

- ❑ Eat a tablespoon of Elmer's Glue (1 point)
- ❑ Have a stranger butter cup a teammate (fart in hand, cup, and bring to mouth and nostrils) (4 points)
- ❑ Get a stranger to do a "mangyna" (tuck dick and balls behind legs) (3 points)
- ❑ Smear mayo all over head and face (2 points)
- ❑ Spank an opponent's Mom (5 points)
- ❑ Put a dildo into your mouth at a sex shop and hum your favorite nursery rhyme (4 points)
- ❑ Find someone whose name is Edgar (2 points)
- ❑ Jump into a ball pit at a Chuck E. Cheese (2 points)
- ❑ Eat a whole piece of jarred gefilte fish (3 points)
- ❑ Get an Emo/Goth/Hipster to say, "I hate my parents." (3 points)
- ❑ Give an Indian burn to an Eastern Indian (4 points)
- ❑ Swim naked in a hotel pool (4 points)
- ❑ Give a Wet Willy to a random person (3 points)
- ❑ Male teammate gets tongue, belly button, or nipple pierced (5 points)
- ❑ Get a white guy above thirty-five to freestyle rap (2 points)
- ❑ Get a little kid to kick you in the nuts (4 points)
- ❑ Climb a tree over twenty-feet-tall (2 points)

- ❑ Find someone with a Tweety Bird bumper sticker **(3 points)**
- ❑ Sit on the hood of a car while going through a car wash **(5 points)**
- ❑ Stuff three pairs of bargain bin panties into your mouth at Victoria's Secret **(5 points)**
- ❑ Swallow a goldfish **(4 points)**
- ❑ Grab a koi fish out of a pond and kiss it **(3 points)**
- ❑ Try three different sexual positions with female partner inside a mattress store **(4 points)**
- ❑ Smoke a cigarette while running on a gym treadmill **(4 points)**
- ❑ Straighten out a wannabe gangster's hat **(2 points)**
- ❑ Get into grocery store freezer **(1 point)**
- ❑ Shave your eyebrows **(5 points)**
- ❑ Glue on moustache of barbershop hair **(2 points)**
- ❑ Jump off of a high dive **(1 point)**
- ❑ Get a male teammate to get a cosmetic counter girl to put on free samples **(2 points)**
- ❑ Thumb wrestle a mailman **(2 points)**
- ❑ Get inside a UPS or ice cream truck **(2 points)**
- ❑ Get someone to show a private area tattoo **(2 points)**
- ❑ Insert your tongue into a bowling ball finger hole **(3 points)**
- ❑ Dip your testicles into a pudding cup inside a grocery store **(4 points)**
- ❑ Smoke a cigarette off the ground **(3 points)**
- ❑ Eat a pube off of a toilet seat **(5 points)**
- ❑ Disintegrate a urinal cake with your bare hands **(4 points)**
- ❑ Do a line of Pixie Stix **(2 points)**
- ❑ Do a stuntman shot at a bar: Snort the salt off your hand, take the shot of tequila and squirt the lime into your eye **(2 points for each team member to do the shot)**
- ❑ Pick a stranger's nose **(2 points)**
- ❑ Smoke a whole cigarette through your nose **(5 points)**
- ❑ Touch a pigeon (much harder than it sounds) **(4 points)**
- ❑ Get a teammate to eat his/her own scab and/or toenail **(1 point)**
- ❑ Get an elderly woman to say, "Can you blow where the Pampers is?" **(3 points)**
- ❑ Have a stranger give you a pink belly **(2 points)**

- ❑ Order a Jamba Juice and pour it down your pants (4 points)
- ❑ Squirt a mayo packet into your mouth (1 point)
- ❑ Two teammates have to eat a cube of butter in under two minutes. (4 points)
- ❑ Play leapfrog with a homeless person (3 points)
- ❑ Get a kiss on the cheek from a meter maid (3 points)
- ❑ Steal a garden gnome (3 points)
- ❑ Find a lemonade stand (1 point)
- ❑ Take a fast pitch batting cage ball in the back (3 points)
- ❑ Take a fast pitch batting cage ball in the chest, Happy Gilmore style (5 points)
- ❑ Do a "Bar Mat Shot": Shot of liquid from spilt drinks resting in rubber mat on top of the bar (4 points)
- ❑ Make a half-court basketball shot (2 points)
- ❑ Make a full-court basketball shot (4 points)
- ❑ Get the life story from a homeless person (3 points)
- ❑ Find someone with a tattoo of a cartoon character (4 points)
- ❑ Jump into a random person's pool (3 points)
- ❑ One teammate has to drink three beers in three minutes (3 points)
- ❑ Eat four home-run pies in under five minutes (2 points)
- ❑ Get someone to quit their job (5 points)
- ❑ Get a stranger to smash a pie in your face (3 points)
- ❑ Get a stranger to smash a pie in his/her face (5 points)
- ❑ Jump off a pier (2 points)
- ❑ Slide head-first into home base (1 points)
- ❑ Get a Mexican guy to juggle a soccer ball ten times (2 points)
- ❑ Jump into a pond (3 points)
- ❑ Find someone named Carl or Todd (2 points)
- ❑ Get a stranger to slap themselves in the face (3 points)
- ❑ Get a stranger to pound a beer and smash it on their forehead (3 points)
- ❑ Convince a stranger to give you his tie (2 points)
- ❑ Sit in a fire truck (3 points)
- ❑ Get a cop to hand-cuff you (5 points)
- ❑ Run through a movie theatre without paying (5 points)

- ❑ Steal someone's air freshener **(2 points)**
- ❑ Steal a gay flag or sticker **(4 points)**
- ❑ Get a girl's phone number **(3 points)**
- ❑ Run across a driving range **(5 points)**
- ❑ Steal someone's golf ball after a hit **(5 points)**
- ❑ Get kicked out of an Applebee's **(4 points)**
- ❑ Find a Nebraska license plate **(2 points)**
- ❑ Get a rollerblader to jump over you while lying down **(3 points)**
- ❑ Whole team does a Whippit in a grocery store **(4 points)**
- ❑ Spot a bald guy in a convertible **(2 points)**
- ❑ Blow a bubble with a condom in your mouth **(2 points)**
- ❑ Get a random guy to give your female teammate a lap dance **(4 points)**
- ❑ Get a person to tell a racial joke about their own race **(3 points)**
- ❑ Kick a thirty-yard field goal **(4 points)**
- ❑ French kiss a woman over sixty **(5 points)**
- ❑ Find someone with a rat tail haircut **(2 points)**
- ❑ Get chased by mall security guard **(4 points)**
- ❑ For every stranger to fake an orgasm on camera (limit five) **(1 point)**
- ❑ Have your female teammate pull pubes out of a stranger's pants **(5 points)**
- ❑ Eat a whole cigarette **(3 points)**
- ❑ Jump through a window of a fast food restaurant **(5 points)**
- ❑ Get Asian tourists to take a picture with you **(3 points)**
- ❑ Eat a piece of binder paper **(2 points)**
- ❑ Convince a stranger to spit in your mouth **(5 points)**
- ❑ Put Nair onto your armpit hair. You must wipe off all hair under your arms **(5 points)**
- ❑ Get a girl to give you her underwear **(4 points)**
- ❑ Buy a porn magazine that is overweight-themed, over-forty-themed, or gay bear–themed **(3 points)**
- ❑ Have a stranger cook you a grilled cheese sandwich **(5 points)**

THE SENIOR CITIZEN GAMES

A senior citizen home is a lot like a college dorm room. Their family members put them there, they take a bunch of drugs, and they have tons of unprotected sex. Hey, we're all going to get old someday, and to tell you the truth, it doesn't sound half bad. Celebrate a time when men had manly names, like Frank and Bruce instead of Cooper and Tristin. Put on some adult diapers, spray paint your hair gray, and pop a few Viagra—it's time to party, senior citizen style.

THE SET-UP

Retirees migrate towards warm weather, so throw the SCG on a warm summer day. Old people are always cooped up in their assisted living homes like prisoners at San Quentin, so find a big backyard or park with plenty of open space for these old timers to stretch their withering legs. Or you could head out for an early bird special since wearing costumes in public places reminds envious onlookers of their own boring existence. Make them jealous of your terry cloth jumpsuit and fake (or real) Viagra boner. You don't have time for judgmental people because you've got a bucket list to accomplish before you croak and still haven't suckled on Edna's B-2 bombers yet.

Senior Citizen Names

- *Abigail*
- *Bruce*
- *Gertrude*
- *Gwendolyn*
- *Harry*
- *Frank*
- *Theodore*
- *Maury*
- *Helen*
- *Prudence*
- *Henriette*
- *Gloria*
- *Edmond*
- *Wilfred*
- *Mortimer*
- *Agnes*
- *Ruth*
- *Mildred*
- *Ethel*
- *Blanche*

DRESS THE PART

Go for the country club aristocrat or the mismatched curmudgeon. Every person should have a costume and a "Hello My Name Is" sticker with a good elderly name (see the following list) and get their hair spray painted gray.

Guys: Elastic-waist pants, Velcro shoes, Hawaiian shirts, fleece cardigans, world's greatest grandpa sweatshirts, plaid golf pants, argyle sweaters, fishing gear, terry cloth bathrobes, short swim trunks with black socks, flannel shirt with overalls, smoking jackets with ascots, and leisure suits. Bonus points if you just wear adult diapers.

Girls: Saggy boobs, mumus, floral print dresses, holiday sweaters, Alfred Dunner clothes (Google it), big dress hats, tennis visors, wrap around side shield sunglasses, large beads, pastel sweatpants, beige grandma panties, nylon tights, shawls, and big beaded jewelry.

STAY ENTERTAINED

Organize a relay race or a tournament with these team games.

Strip Bocce Ball: Bocce ball is won by getting seven points. Every time a team scores a point, the other team has to remove one article of clothing (hats, shoes, socks, and accessories are included). Seven points should get you right down to the skivvies (Bingo Shuffleboard and Lawn Darts could be played as well).

Tapioca Pudding Eating Competition: Teams of four have to finish tapioca pudding like a boat race.

Depends Wheelchair/Wheelbarrow Race: Teammates have to switch adult diapers before each leg of the race.

Putt-Putt Competition: Buy a pair of really magnified prescription glasses from your local drugstore. Each player has to wear the thick glasses (beer goggles), spin five times on the putter, and then try to sink the shot.

Wii Bowling Tournament: Lowest bowling score has to wear the Depends diapers for the remainder of the party.

Water Aerobics: Senior ladies love one-piece swimsuits and water aerobics. Have the girls choreograph a dance to Glenn Miller's "In the Mood."

Keep it old school when it comes to beverage choices. Try a Tom Collins, White Russian, or Vodka Gimlet.

Tom Collins

1½ ounces gin
2 ounces sweet-and-sour mix
club soda to fill
orange slice and cherry

Combine gin and sweet-and-sour mix in a shaker. Shake and strain into a Collins glass of ice. Fill with club soda. Garnish with an orange and cherry.

White Russian

1 ounce Kahlúa
1 ounce vodka
2 ounces cream

Shake all ingredients and pour into a short glass of ice.

Vodka Gimlet

2 ounces vodka
½ ounce Rose's lime juice
lime wedge

Add all ingredients to a mixing glass half filled with ice. Shake and strain into a rocks glass of ice. Garnish with lime wedge.

SMOKING GUN PARTY

The Smoking Gun is a website that posts legal documents, arrest records, and celebrity mugshots. It is also a great theme for a house party. Send out an invite with the list of celebrity mugshots from the website. Have partygoers reserve a celebrity they will imitate. Each celebrity can only be used once, unless they select Lohan, who has been arrested for multiple offenses.

THE SET-UP

Buy black poster board and white markers to make mugshot placards for everyone. The placards include name, city of arrest, and violation. Organize the drinking games (trials) according to arrest violations. For example, wife beaters play Flip Cup against marijuana possessions, while DUIs challenge the cocaine offenders to a game of anchorman. Separate into teams according to the celebrity violation. Losing team of celebrity offenders should be handcuffed together and sent to the jail (bathroom/garage) to finish an allocated amount of alcohol. The winners beat their trials and get to continue partying.

The Suspect Lineup

CELEBRITY	BUSTED FOR . . .	COSTUME IDEA
Anna Nicole Smith	Drunk Driving	Get a bunch of candy and put in a prescription bottle. Eat them like popcorn and wash down with straight vodka.
Yasmine Bleeth	Cocaine Possession	Red Baywatch top and cover your face in powdered sugar.
Mel Gibson	Drunk Driving	*Braveheart* face paint with a bottle of tequila in your kilt.
Michael Vick	Dog Fighting	Michael Vick jersey with a do-rag. Don't forget to buy a stuffed dog and pull it around with you.
Tonya Harding	Assault	Ice-skating singlet, tights, rollerblades and don't forget your Kerrigan beating stick.
Kobe Bryant	Sexual Assault	Kobe jersey then duct tape a blonde blowup doll to your waist.
Lindsay Lohan	Cocaine Possession	Anything that shows off your freckled tits.
Matthew McConaughey	Marijuana possession and playing the bongos naked	Wear tighty-whities and bongos around your waist. Make sure to speak with the McConaugha-twang all night.
Steve-O	Indecent Exposure or stapling your scrotum to your thigh at a bar	Aviator glasses, draw a picture of yourself on your back, and get creative by somehow making a fake ball sack.
Nick Nolte	Drunk Driving	The mother of all mugshots. Wear a Hawaiian shirt and electrocute yourself a few times. If possible, don't sleep for forty-eight hours before the party.

SUNDAY FUNDAY

Most weekend warriors pull back on the reins as soon as the seventh day rolls around. Why not take a rain check on that colossal headache by taking advantage of something called the shampoo effect? All it takes is one beer and an inspirational speech by a peer to transform a day of painful headaches and moaning into a memorable occasion awesome Sunday Funday. See if you can follow this alcoholic logic. You're going to be miserable on Monday, whether you're hungover or not, so you might as well consolidate the misery of a Sunday hangover with the misery of Monday—it's going to suck anyway. Genius. Here are some of our Sunday Funday staples.

THE SET-UP

There really isn't any set-up for a Sunday Funday. It's just you and a close group of friends riding that hangover out through some entertaining day drinking. Here are some games and activities to help roll your hangover to Monday.

InnerTube Water Polo

Have more of a lean-over than a hangover? Then have an active Sunday Funday. Wash away Saturday night with some light aqua-cise. Visit *www.innertubewaterpolo.com* for official rules.

Lean-over: A medium-sized hangover.

Mini NFL Helmet Challenge

Each player gets two mini helmets from the outdoor toy dispensers at grocery stores. Teams can be picked more than once, but teams with a bi-week, playing Sunday night or Monday night do not count. Every player then puts in $10 to $20 for the pot. After all the games, the player that has the highest combined point score wins "beaucoup money bitches."

Taco Bell Draft

Find five friends, buy forty different items from the menu, and bring them home. Write each item on a whiteboard or large piece of paper. Like a fantasy football draft, competitors take turns picking/crossing off choices. Once every player has eight items, the referee starts a countdown. The first player to finish all eight of his items is declared champion. Then have fistfights for dibs on the shitter.

Broom Ball

Broom ball is essentially hockey played on a rink, in shoes, and using brooms instead of sticks and a ball instead of a puck. Most ice rinks will rent the materials.

Skee-Ball Tourney

Venture out and find skeeball at your local arcade or dive bar. Split into teams of two and pick a team name (The Skee-Amigos, Skee-Bags, Skee6 Mafia, All Skee Skee Motherfuckers, Skee-Lows, Skee-Melio Estevez, Sha-skee O'Neals, or the Flock of Skee-Gulls). Have a tournament and make the loosing team get spray-on tans. Make sure to use the Playboy bunny stickers too.

DECISIONS, DECISIONS

Hungover in a living room with friends and need some hilarious conversation starters? These questions are sure to keep you entertained as you keep the headache at bay.

1. Would you rather ring out Rosie O'Donnell's grandma panties after she's been on a long jog in garbage bags and take a shot of the gray liquid or watch your mother make out with a homeless person?

2. Would you rather throw a hand grenade into a bin of golden retriever puppies or cover every orifice of Oprah's body in mayo and lick it all off?

3. Would you rather eat a sandwich of John Lithgow's chest hair or drink a chilled martini of Amy Winehouse's stomach bile?

4. Would you rather make love to Megan Fox once and go impotent for the rest of your life or get butt-fucked by Flavor Flav and have naturally induced Viagra dick for the rest of your life?

5. Would you rather live in a studio apartment with Suge Knight or Gary Busey?

6. Would you rather have your parents watch you have sex or watch your parents have sex?

7. Would you rather have to watch *Jurassic Park* every day for a year or stomp a raccoon to death with steel-toe boots?

8. Would you rather go down on Barbra Streisand until she orgasms or watch your girlfriend give Richard Grieco a rusty trombone?

9. Would you rather eat a spoonful of cinnamon after every time you have sex or uncontrollably shart your pants every time you hear a Mariah Carey song?

10. Would you rather get one lap dance from Eva Mendes or get super stoned with Dave Chappelle and play *Grand Theft Auto* for a whole day?

11. Would you rather your sister marry one of the Gotti boys or you lose all hair on your body except for a Hitler moustache?

12. Would you rather never be able to watch a football game ever again or give up both cheese *and* bacon?

13. Would you rather party with George Clooney for a whole summer at his Lake Como villa or be the road manager for a Kings of Leon tour?

14. Would you rather be stuck in a secluded mountain cabin with Dave Matthews, a guitar, and a bunch of heroin or gangbang Joan Rivers with the Wu Tang Clan?

15. Would you rather change your name to Spiderman Shitstain or Melky Cumstein?

16. Would you rather masturbate on a stage in front of every one of your childhood teachers while being shot with BB Guns or be sentenced to one day in a maximum-security prison?

17. Would you rather get Tupac's "Thug Life" AK-47 tattoo on your stomach or get a tattoo of a praying nun on the underside of your penis (with your head as hers)?

18. Would you rather wake up tomorrow and be a really good-looking Korean woman or be yourself and have no front teeth and a permanent unibrow?

19. Would you rather drink forties and shoot machine guns at brand new cars with 50 Cent or have a weekend movie marathon with Quentin Tarantino and all of your best friends?

20. Would you rather have a threesome with Angelina Jolie and Jennifer Anniston and never be able to tell anyone or sleep with Rosie O'Donnell and have everyone know about it but buy you free beer just to hear the story?

21. Would you rather tattoo a six-pack of Pabst Blue Ribbon on your stomach or tattoo a gang symbol across your back?

22. Would you rather get in a fistfight with Justin Bobby from *The Hills* or Carrot Top?

23. Would you rather be at a swanky Hollywood cocktail party and kick Mini-Me as hard as you can in front of a crowd of people or cover your naked body in Crisco and streak through the Macy's Thanksgiving Day Parade?

24. Would you rather re-enact the movie *Misery* with you as James Caan and Andy Dick as Kathy Bates or re-enact the tent scene from *Brokeback Mountain* with you and Yao Ming?

25. Would you rather convince Carls Jr. to name a burger after your grandfather or co-write a shitty movie with Bruce Campbell?

26. Would you rather wake up tomorrow and look like Susan Boyle but be able time travel or wake up and look like Ryan Reynolds and run a booze-cruise in Cabo San Lucas?

27. Would you rather have your intoxication level magically linked to Lil Wayne's or get date raped by the entire cast of hobbits in their *Lord of the Rings* costumes?

28. Would you rather be stuck in a Toys 'R US with ten friends for forty-eight hours and all you can eat is pot brownies or would you rather have an unlimited tab for one night at the Spearmint Rhino in Las Vegas but you have to go by yourself?

29. Would you rather be queefed on by Queen Latifah or peed on by Pee Wee Herman?

30. Would you rather have an entourage of Hells Angels follow you everywhere or vomit every time someone uses the phrase, "in and of itself." (Be sure to consider Thanksgiving dinner conversations and business meetings.)

31. Would you rather hang out with Jack White and fifteen Suicide Girls in a Savannah Georgia mansion while he records a new album or be able to beat any challenger in a dunk competition?

32. Would you rather have carrot sticks have the same affect as ecstasy pills only for you or be able to moonwalk as well as Michael Jackson?

33. Would you rather go back in time and prevent one sexual encounter or be able to eat free at Applebee's forever?

34. Would you rather go to Ibiza on private plane with Daft Punk or go to Burning Man in a shitty Winnebago with Brad Pitt?

35. Would you rather be visited by the ghost of Hunter S. Thompson and do acid with him at Disneyland or be visited by the ghost of John Belushi, finish a bottle of jack and get into a cannonball competition?

36. Would you rather be able to karaoke any song perfectly or never have to pay for a cab ride again?

37. Would you rather be responsible for solving the Israel Palestinian conflict or sign a deal that Universal and Steven Spielberg have to make every one of your movie ideas?

38. Would you rather wake up tomorrow and be Snooki from *The Jersey Shore* or wake up and tomorrow and be yourself only your eyes and nipples have switched places?

39. Would you rather be a famous artist who only paints in their own blood and urine or have to end every day of your life by watching an episode of *The Hills*?

40. Would you rather have super hero powers but could only use them when you and your friends were blackout drunk or would you be really famous underwear model in Japan?

41. Would you rather wake up every morning to encouraging personal voice mails from Morgan Freeman or do mocaine (mushrooms and cocaine) and go surfing with Matthew McConaughey?

42. Would you rather convince Steve Jobs to invest in your virtual reality porn company or would you rather be able to cast any stars and supporting cast in your life story?

43. Would you rather be able to poke one of Salma Hayek's turtleneck boobs or get a shout out in T-Pain's next hit single?

44. Would you rather have the ability to have your house clean itself after parties simply by sitting cross legged and meditating or always smell like you just took a shower?

45. Would you rather have hangovers completely erased from your life or never sit in traffic ever again?

46. Would you be Courtney Love's personal love slave gimp for a year or film a homeless person male-on-male porno called *Bum Cum 4*?

47. Would you rather get Ed Hardy shirt tattooed on your whole upper body or close your eyes and take one right cross from Chuck Liddel?

48. Would you rather wake up tomorrow and only be sexually attracted to women over 60 or have your Mom start dating your best friend?

49. Would you rather fly to Brazil and get a sex change or play Russian Roulette once?

50. Would you rather be allowed to drink only on federal holidays or any day between the hours of 10 A.M. to 1 P.M.?

KEEP THE SUNDAY FUNDAY GOING AND COME UP WITH SOME OF YOUR OWN. EVEN IF YOU THOUGHT YOU KNEW YOUR FRIENDS, THESE PROMPTS WILL BRING SOME NEW THINGS TO LIGHT—ESPECIALLY IF EVERYONE'S RELIT SATURDAY'S FIRE.

TOMA TODO! A CINCO DE DRINKO DINNER PARTY

You gotta love American business. They turned J-Dawg's resurrection into an egg hunt and they turned an anti-imperialist Mexican struggle (Cinco de Mayo) into a college drinking day. Good job Corona marketing team!

THE SET-UP

Don't let Cinco de Drinko pass you by without some tequila-induced tabletop dancing. Just follow these simple steps and you will be adios pantalones drunk.

The Dinner Guests

Make each guest responsible for bringing a case of Mexican beer, a bottle of tequila, and $10 worth of quarters. If you have 401ks, then you rich bastards can play with dollar bills.

Host's Duties

The host should be responsible for chips, salsa, and a wide variety of tamales. Find them locally or cop out and go to Trader Joe's.

The Games

Notice a pattern by this point? We pick a theme (like Mexico) then proceed to come up with drinking games that both celebrate and stereotype the topic of choice.

Toma Todo!

Toma Todo (translates to "take it all") is not Lil Wanye's drug mantra. It's a kickass drinking game played with a dreidel, a bunch of quarters, and tequila—of course.

Order an official six-sided tomo toda dreidel, or steal one from your Jewish friend's house while his family is watching *Curb Your Enthusiasm* and label the dreidel (good Jewish rap song):

Side 1: Toma Uno (Take one quarter from the pot.)

Side 2: Toma Dos (Take two quarters from the pot.)

Side 3: Toma Todo! (Yell, "Toma todo!" Then take the whole pot and a shot of tequila.)

Side 4: Pon Uno (Put one quarter in the pot.)

Side 5: Pon Dos (Put two quarters in the pot.)

Side 6: Todos Ponen (Everyone puts two quarters in the pot.)

You can play Toma Todo with just alcohol, but it's much more fun to win $15 worth of quarters. You will have laundry money for months. *Note:* If you are a poor college kid and can't afford good booze, do tequila poppers. Fill half a shot glass with tequila and the other half with 7-Up. Put a rag over the glass and slam it down onto a hard countertop. Quickly take the shot. The carbonation will fizz to the top and eradicate the ashtray flavor from your plastic jug of tequila.

Mexican Train Game

It sounds like a game at an '80s swingers' party, but it's basically a different version of dominoes. The game is a blast and creates plenty of opportunities for sexual innuendos. Buy it. It's $15 at Target.

The Chelada Challenge

If you blended a pint of ocean water, a dead fish, and two tomatoes you would have the same recipe as Budweiser's Chelada. The King of Beers created this horrendous concoction in a desperate effort to tap into the emerging Hispanic market. What can we say? We're hooked on this disgusting beverage. We can't go to the liquor store without buying one for a little game we call the Chelada Challenge—the perfect game for a large group of people during Cinco de Drinko festivities.

The Rules

1. Everyone playing gets one die.
2. Each round, all players roll their dice once at the same time.
3. If you roll a six, you are out of the competition and a new round starts for those that did not roll a six.
4. The last player to not roll a six has to drink the twenty-four ounces of Mexican Sailor Piss.

QUOTES FROM PAST CHELADA DRINKERS

"It tasted like a hangover. It was a sour tomato soupy mess that made me want to reseal the can and bury it at the center of the earth to put it beyond the reach of likewise curious folks. If you're a glutton for punishment, or your curiosity must be satisfied at all cost, I still have two cans taking up space in my fridge."—hoosierbeergeek.blogspot.com

ANY GAME CAN WORK AS A CHELADA CHALLENGE, AS LONG AS THE PUNISHMENT FOR LOSING OR BREAKING A RULE IS ALWAYS THE DELICIOUS CHELADA.

TOUR DE FRANZIA

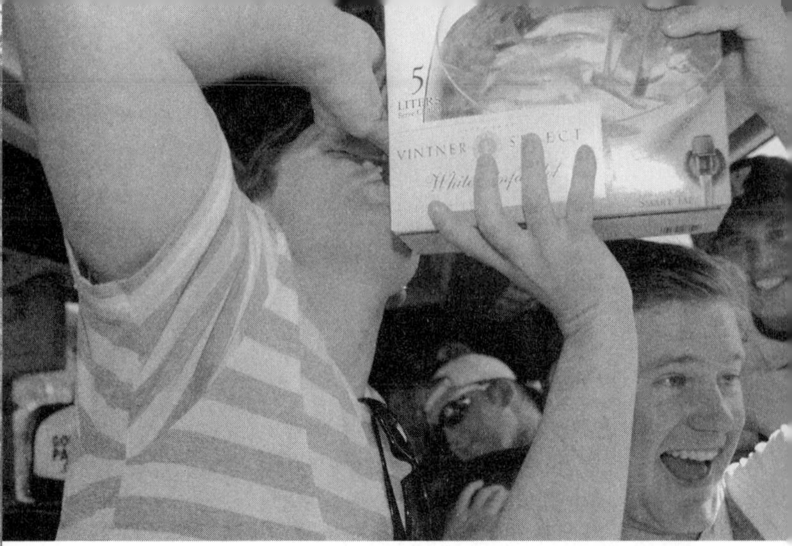

Nothing screams dirty Frenchmen better than spandex shorts and boxed wine. The Tour de Franzia is a fail-proof idea if you're looking to drink on the move, spill on yourself, and scrape your knees in the process. This is a progressive party, which means as you move from each drinking location (house or bar) you pick up new members.

THE SET-UP

Everyone should be required to carry one or two bags of wine in his backpack. Camel packs are a luxury, but at the first meeting spot, partygoers should try to get creative with duct tape and tubing to see who can construct the best drinking mechanism. Hand out the Google map directions of your pub crawl. If you live in a big city or small college town, mix in houses to stop at and pick up other racers. As you pass strangers yell, "Bonjour!" And then offer them Franzia. Try to get them to join you on your pub crawl.

DRESS THE PART

Get to your local thrift store or costume shop and buy used spandex biking outfits. Biker shorts are mandatory but exposed fruit cups and camel toes are not. Buy extra shirts so you can invite random people to join you along the way. Headgear is mandatory. Each participant should have on a bike helmet or beret. (Berets are cheap, so buy extra.) Thin French Sharpie-moustachios are also required for guys. If you don't have a Sharpie handy, you can use a burnt wine cork.

Warning: Drinking and biking is dangerous and against the law. This doesn't mean it isn't a fun pastime if done safely. If you do ride bikes, stay off the main roads. Keep the bike riding to someone's yard or in a park. Wearing spandex shorts in the drunk-tank will not be a high point in your life.

STAY ENTERTAINED

Stop in a public park to play one of these activities:

For the main event, have a piggyback relay race with guys carrying girls. Before each leg of the race, the participant has to take a pull from the Franzia bag.

Hold a blindfolded French bread fight.

Organize a giant game of Duck, Duck, Goose. Trust us. After a few sunset blush Franzias, this will be a blast. "Now get in the goddamn mush pot! It's time to play Duck, Duck, Goose!"

Find two brave souls to see who can smoke a cigarette faster while making weird Frenchy sounds. Bonus points if done through the nose.

Since the French are known for inventing oral pleasures, split into two lines of players, break out a credit card, and see which team can score the Suck and Blow victory.

When the party hits ludicrous speed start doing some "long-distance Franz." Hold the bag of wine like a bagpipe against your side and squeeze the bag between your arm and your side, causing the Franzia to shoot out in a stream. The receiver has to catch the Franzia in a cup on his head. The total amount of Franzia is measured and the losing team has to drink both cups of Franz.

The next logical step is to turn the Franzia boxes into hats and continue to the last leg of your race.

TOURIST PARTY

If you have ever lived in a large city, you probably know how fun it is to give directions to Chinatown when an obnoxious family from Arkansas is trying to find the Hard Rock Cafe. Then you try to keep a straight face as the troglodytes waddle away holding their tourist maps. But don't feel one baby dick of remorse for these Ranch-hounds. These people travel abroad and give good Americans a bad name. So let's do what we do best and throw a politically incorrect party making fun of obnoxious American tourists.

THE SET-UP

Lots of big cities in the United States have sightseeing tour buses. Either hop aboard one of the guided tours or rent out your own bus. If you rent your own bus, make sure to actually stop at famous landmarks between bars so you can take big group pictures. Your pub crawl should take you through the most bars at big chain restaurants (Applebee's, T.G.I.Friday's, Red Robin, Planet Hollywood, Bubba Gumps, Chili's, and especially the Hard Rock Cafe), where you will be surrounded by patrons who look just like you.

How to Act like an Obnoxious Tourist

- *Continually ask the bartender for sides of ranch dressing.*
- *Randomly scream "I love waffle fries!" every half hour.*
- *Keep requesting the bar to play Jimmy Buffett songs.*
- *Ask everyone to take pictures for you.*
- *Continually start sentences with the phrase, "Well, where I come from . . . ."*

DON'T FORGET TO HANG YOUR CAMERA AROUND YOUR NECK AND THROW ON SOME WRAPAROUND SUNGLASSES.

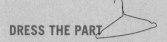

DRESS THE PART

Partygoers are responsible for their own tourist t-shirt from the city you are pretending to visit. Girls should wear visors and guys should sport NFL hats. Everyone should have a fanny pack or backpack (for your sunscreen, Doritos, and city maps). And jean shorts are mandatory for both men and women. To finish off the look, wear striped tube-socks and sandals, water socks, or brand-new white tennis shoes.

STAY ENTERTAINED

As you're bar hopping, keep the fun going with some trivia about Americans' favorite subject—fatty foods.

1. How many pounds of potato chips do Americans consume every year?
Answer: Two billion

2. What is the Twinkie defense?
Answer: Claims that the effect of coffee, nicotine, allergies, or sugar entered into the motives of the crime.

3. Which candy bar was named after the family horse? a) Snickers b) Butterfinger c) Milky Way
Answer: Snickers

4. How did Procter and Gamble choose the name Pringles?
Answer: Picked it from a phone book.

5. What does Doritos mean in Spanish?
A) golden crackers B) cheesy chips
C) little bits of gold
Answer: Little bits of gold

UNITED NATIONS PARTY

Global Warming, conflict in the Middle East, gay baby seals dying due to second-hand smoke . . . there's only one way to settle these pressing world issues—the United Nations Party.

THE SET-UP

The point of the party is to create a microcosm of global politics by substituting oil with keg beer. Prior to your United Nations Party, have your friends randomly select country names out of a hat. Give them a week or so to find good costumes.

The OPEC (Organization of Petroleum Exporting Countries) characters are in charge of the kegs. The standard party should have four OPEC members in charge of four different kegs. (If you're really going all out, there are twelve members of OPEC.) Each OPEC member has a camera and a list of embarrassing challenges and tasks for thirsty U.N. members to perform before receiving alcohol.

Costumes for OPEC Members

- *Nigeria: Brightly colored dashikis, matching African caps*
- *Saudi Arabia: Keffiyehs (Arab headdresses), white robes, Mercedes Benz bling, and aviators*
- *Iran: Tight black pants, gold rings, striped shirts, mandatory Bluetooth, fake moustaches, and an excessive amount of designer cologne*
- *Venezuela: Soccer jerseys, extreme partying club sunglasses, whistles, short athletic shorts, tennis shoes, and a ton of hair gel*

*If you need more OPEC members (kegs), the other eight countries in the alliance are Algeria, Angola, Ecuador, Iraq, Kuwait, Libya, Qatar, and the United Arab Emirates.

DRINKING GAME GRUDGE MATCHES

All drinking games (Beer Pong, Flip Cup, Speed Quarters, or Anchorman) must be played with allies against historical enemies. Here are the best matchups:

- *WWII Beer Pong: USA and England vs. Germany and Japan*
- *Rape of Nanking Grudge Match: China vs. Japan*
- *Friendly Cousins Match: Ireland vs. Australia*
- *1967 Grudge Match: Israel vs. Egypt (Israel gets to start with two turns)*
- *World Cup Grudge Match: Brazil vs. Argentina*
- *Beer Drinkers Grudge Match: Canada vs. Austria*
- *Rum Drinking Grudge Match: Bahamas vs. Barbados*
- *Olive Oil Cup: Italy vs. Greece*
- *1,000-Yard Stare Match: Russia vs. Japan*
- *OPEC Grudge Match #1: Iran vs. Saudi Arabia*
- *OPEC Grudge Match #2: Nigeria vs. Venezuela*

*Jamaica purposely left out due to lack of motivation to move from the couch.

PLAY THE PART

Depending on the number of people coming to your United Nations Party, individuals or groups of people can represent countries. Also remember the *South Park* rule: It's not offensive as long as you offend everyone. Don't leave anyone out.

COUNTRY	COSTUME
Argentina	Soccer jerseys and mullet wigs
Australia	Rugby jersey, black eyes, board shorts, bikinis, bathing suits, and scrumcaps
Austria	Arnold merchandise and or lederhosen
Bahamas	Tropical clothes and straw hats
Bermuda	Bright polos and Bermuda shorts
Brazil	Swimsuits, tropical clothes, fake tanner, and carnival masks
Canada	Hockey jerseys with a blacked-out tooth or a Canadian Mounties uniform
China	Rice hats and black slippers
Egypt	Pharaohs and Cleopatras
France	Black-and-white striped shirts with berets
Greece	Togas and laurels
India	Saris with bindis
Ireland	Wool caps, black eyes, and anything green
Israel	Yarmulkes and Groucho Marx glasses
Italy	Wife beaters with marinara stains, gold crosses, and designer jeans.
Jamaica	Dreadlocks and mesh tank tops
Japan	Short black wigs with lab coats or Kabuki outfits
Mexico	Ponchos and sombreros
Russian	Fur hats and red Adidas sweatsuits
Switzerland	Referee outfits (Switzerland must solve all beer game quarrels)
England	Sweater vests, three-piece tweed suits, long pleated skirts
United States	Cowboys hats and NASCAR/WWE/NFL shirts

'Check out the U.N.'s Wikipedia page if you need more countries to fill out your international festivities.

THE VIETNAM VET PARTY

Disclaimer: 5th Year has nothing but respect for veterans. This party was actually submitted by a U.S. Marine Corps Captain who did three tours in Iraq. (Thanks, Brian.) This is not meant to mock servicemen. This party is a celebration of the fact that having a sense of humor has always been a cornerstone of the American military.

THE SET-UP

The Vietnam Vet party is a backyard Burning Man meets *Apocalypse Now*. Can you think of anything better than loud classic rock, day-drinking, and girls in sexy cheongsam dresses? If not, "I bet you're the kind of guy that would fuck a person in the ass and not even have the goddamn common courtesy to give him a reach-around!"

The key to the Vietnam Vet Party is warm weather and a big open space (camping site or backyard). Go all out, maggots!

OVER THE TOP

Have people bring tents and make it an overnight party. That's when you can get your special lady, "to love you long time."

DRESS THE PART

Guys: Military camouflage; handle bar moustaches, red bandanas, fake tattoos, rock-and-roll t-shirts, dog tags, horn-rimmed glasses, and toy guns. Or just keep it simple and go in white boxers, combat boots, and a helmet.

Costume Ideas
Forrest Gump

Lieutenant Dan
(wheelchair recommended)

Lt. Colonel Kilgore
(Robert Duvall, *Apocalypse Now*)

The pacifist war photographer

Animal Mother or Joker
(*Full Metal Jacket*)

Girls: Help out our boys by donning nurse uniforms or going the flashy route with revealing USO girl outfits.

STAY ENTERTAINED

Keep in the wartime spirit by playing Minefield. The game is played with two teams of two (that makes four). One teammate is blindfolded at the starting line while one teammate is yelling directions from the finish line. Grab ten other friends to act as the stationary mines. Each mine has some type of punishment: noogies, wet willies, full beer chugs, atomic wedgies, or shots. The blindfolded contestants try to make their way through the minefield just from the verbal directions of their teammate. If they are tagged by one of the stationary mines they have to take the punishment then continue to navigate through the field. First person to cross the finish line wins.

CHALK IT UP

Like a military operation, the danger of a night out can escalate pretty quickly. How many nights have you lied to yourself and your friends with the statement, "Don't worry, we'll just go out and get a few drinks"? You arrive to the bar as normal patrons but around the four-drink tipping point, there is collective decision to turn up the fun meter. This is usually cemented by ordering a round of shots, which signifies, "Hey we tricked ourselves into coming out, we might as well make the most of it." Then all it takes is a simple chalk mustache to snowball into a DEFCON Level 5 night of debauchery. Here's how Chalk It Up works.

DEFCON Level 1: Hey, you know what would be funny if we took that pool cue chalk over there and made ourselves Smurf beards.

DEFCON Level 2: Everyone gets chalked + more Pabst + chalk handlebar mustache arm wrestling tournament.

DEFCON Level 3: We are now officially shitfaced. The most logical thing to do is go into public and create chalk body outlines in sexual positions.

DEFCON Level 4: Go to another bar. Chalk up willing patrons. Scare the other half.

DEFCON Level 5: Draw dead body chalk scenes complete with chalk penises.

Next time you're at a bar with your friends, remember to Chalk It Up.

PLAYLIST

"Run Through the Jungle"
Creedence Clearwater Revival

"Long Cool Woman (In Black Dress)"
The Hollies

"Paint It, Black"
The Rolling Stones

"Surfin' Bird"
The Ramones

"Baby, Please Don't Go"
Them

"All Along the Watchtower"
Jimi Hendrix

"Born in the U.S.A."
Bruce Springsteen

"Fortunate Son"
Creedence Clearwater Revival

"Charlie Don't Surf"
The Clash

"The Unknown Soldier"
The Doors

PARTY BONUS POINTS FOR SMOKING OUT OF TOY GUNS, HAVING PARTYGOERS DO THE PLATOON COVER POSE WITH AN EMPTY KEG, HOT-BOXING YOUR TENT, AND CONVINCING THE GIRLS TO DO A FASHION SHOW WALK TO NANCY SINATRA'S "THESE BOOTS ARE MADE FOR WALKING."

WEDDING CRASHERS: BACHELORETTE PARTY EDITION

Do you really want to spend your last single night drinking rum out of a plastic penis while watching a glitterly Puerto Rican grind on your girlfriends? For most bachelorette parties, the bride-to-be is nervous about stories leaking out and her bridesmaids are just using her as an excuse to get debauchilicious. Here is a win-win situation that is sure to create some good pictures.

Debauchilicious: When a girl decides to get scandalous after consuming many alcoholic beverages.

THE SET-UP

Tell the bride she will be picked up and to wear a cute outfit. Have the girls in the bachelorette party go to a vintage store and buy the ugliest wedding gowns they can find. Show up in the dresses and surprise the bride. Instead of the fiancée embarrassing herself, it sets the stage for the bridesmaids to show her the kind of reckless inebriation that she will be glad to leave behind.

STAY ENTERTAINED

The maid of honor should provide the bride with a pair of safety scissors and a stack of note cards with challenges for her bridal party. (You can print out the full list at *www.5thYear.com*.) The bride gets to issue challenges to her girlfriends. If they don't succeed or decide to pass on the challenge, the bride gets to cut off a piece of her wedding gown. If the bridal party wants to stay presentable, they will have to comply with bridezilla's demands.

Note Card Challenges

- ❑ Do a shot without using your hands.
- ❑ Get the bouncer to give you a piggyback ride around the bar.
- ❑ Get a guy to buy the bridal party a round of shots.
- ❑ Flubber a guy's stomach (done by pressing one's mouth against it, exhaling, and making a fart-like noises).
- ❑ Dance on the bar.
- ❑ Convince a guy to do a bar mat shot.
- ❑ Fake an orgasm in the bar.
- ❑ Convince a guy to let you read his text messages.
- ❑ Convince a guy to drunk-dial a random number on his phone.
- ❑ Make a guy wear lipstick.
- ❑ Quiet the bar and give a toast.
- ❑ Convince the DJ to play Madonna's "Like a Prayer."
- ❑ Convince a guy to let the bride give him a wedgie.
- ❑ Do a body shot on the bar.
- ❑ The bride can update any bridesmaid's Facebook status using someone's BlackBerry or iPhone.
- ❑ The bride picks out a guy and the girl has to give him a rejection hotline number.
- ❑ The bride picks two bridesmaids to have a dance off to a song of her choice.
- ❑ Do a finger mustache photo (draw a mustache on the inside of one's index finger and place it over the upper lip).
- ❑ Get a group of guys to do the Zoolander pose with the bride.
- ❑ Do a Chilly Willy shot (ingest alcohol through the nose via snorting; often done out of the concave bottom of a shot glass).

WHIP IT! ROLLER DERBY PARTY

If you haven't seen Drew Barrymore's kick-ass roller derby movie *Whip It!*, starring Ellen Page, rent it now. Just like the real roller derby, it has something for everyone: ruthless competition, hot suicide girls in fishnets, and hilarious characters. Roller derby is the fastest growing sport right now, with five hundred and eighteen teams worldwide, ranging from the L.A. Derby Dolls to the Berlin Bombshells. It's time for you and your friends to strap on your skates and be your own hero. The Whip It! Roller Derby Party is perfect for a sorority fundraiser or your girlfriend's no-tears-allowed birthday party.

THE SET-UP

The first step is to rent a roller rink or a community center with a basketball court. Either surface can be used to play roller derby. Then, as long as the 2012 Mayan Apocalypse hasn't rendered Google useless, you should be able to find the rules online. Look up "Women's Flat Track Derby Association."

Have two guys be the referees for the night and appoint another funny friend to be the announcer, a.k.a. "Hot-Tub" Johnny.

Prior to the party, have the girls organize into teams of five. Each team should have two to three male coaches, so that both sexes can be involved. The coach's responsibilities are to diagram plays, drink out of flasks, and give overly dramatic pump-up speeches. Male coaches are also required to wear short colorful athletics shorts, high striped socks, and headbands. If you want your girls to take you seriously, you've go to look the part.

Each team should decide who'll fill the following positions: one jammer (scorer), three blockers (defense), and one pivot (a blocker who may become the jammer later in that jam). Each team also has to come up with the following: team name, team costume, and individual player names. Get creative and invent your own or use one of these examples.

Existing Team Names That Don't Suck

- *The Anti-Socialites*
- *The Backwood Betties*
- *The Brawlarinas*
- *The Death Leopard*
- *The Empire Skate Troopers*
- *Full Metal Corsets*
- *Gang Green*
- *The Glamazons*
- *Green Barrettes*
- *Hades Ladies*
- *The Ho-Bots*
- *The Killopatras*
- *The Rattle Skates*
- *The Rabid Bambies*
- *The Rollitas*
- *Secretaries of the Skate*
- *Skates on a Plane*
- *St. Brawli Girls*
- *Suffra Jets*
- *The Trampires*
- *The Unicorn Punchers*

EXISTING PLAYER NAMES THAT KICK ASS

Quarter-Pound Her

AC Skater

Abita Hoedown

Affirmative Smaction

Agatha Frisky

Al Punchino

Allison Wonderslam

Amelia No-Heart

Buns and Ammo

Babe Ruthless

Baberaham Lincoln

BackBlock Obama

Bam-Bam Larue

Battle Star Kick-astica

Betty-Aim-Fire

Blaze N. Confused

Buckingham Malice

Carnage Electra

Chesty McBruiser

Chow-Mean

Christina Scrapplegate

Chuck E. Sleeze

Clitty Clitty Bang Bang

Dakota Slamming

Deadliest Snatch

Domaskatrix

Dora the Destroyer

Ellen De Generate

Erin Blockabitch

Fidela Castrate

Halle Scary

Hurrican Skatrina

Injury Anna Jones

Killary Clinton

and Lady Harmalade

WHEN PICKING YOUR ROLLER DERBY NAME IT'S GOT TO BE SEXY BUT ALSO HAVE SOME MOXY. YOU WANT IT TO SAY, I'M GOING TO LOOK GOD-DAMN DELICIOUS IN FISHNETS BUT ALSO SCREAM I'M READY TO THROW SOME BOWS. COSTUME ACCESSORIES ENCOURAGED.

THE WILLIAM WALLACE INVITATIONAL

To most, golf is synonymous with concentration and tranquility. For 5th Year, it means kilts, drinking pints of ale, and painting your face while yelling "Freedom!" at the foursome in front of you. The William Wallace Invitational is perfect for a birthday or bachelor party while paying respect to the fact that golf was invented in Scotland.

THE SET-UP

The key to this event is finding the right course. Don't get too cocky and try to organize the WWI at a snobby country club. Stay away from anywhere that costs more than $20 to play. You'll end up getting arrested by the local magistrate (police) and sentenced to a night in the dungeon (drunk tank). Go public. Plan for the event to be nine holes.

You could try to rent the whole course for a few hours, but if you can't afford it—go guerrilla style.

Players must find and wear kilts (or use a plaid bed sheet if you want to go the cheap route). This is the corner stone to the outfit. What's great about the kilt is you can very easily flash your opponents, frontal or backside. It's a sign of Scottish confidence . . . I guess. In true *Braveheart* fashion, players must wear the decorative blue battle paint on their faces. This strikes fear into the strokes of your opponents . . . just when you are about to sink a putt, imagine a group of Highlanders from the MacGregor clan screaming and flashing their bagpipes—it's a going to be a pressure cooker out there.

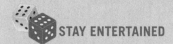

STAY ENTERTAINED

You could be boring and play a normal round of golf, but we would never suggest that. You have nine holes to play with; shoot it straight for a few holes then dick around on the rest:

Throw Your Ball Round
"The English won't let us train with weapons, so we train with stones . . . ." Every player must throw their ball into the hole. Replace strokes with throws.

Putter Only Round
No need for an explanation.

Polo with Partners Round
You get on your partners back. The guy on back hits the ball polo style. The guy holding then runs to the ball. You switch, and hit, and run. First to sink the ball wins.

Braveheart *Round*
Every time you hit the ball you have to recite a different *Braveheart* quote. First to repeat a quote or miss a quote has to finish his beer.

Shot-put Round
At hole eight, fill a thirty-pack box with finished cans. Duct tape the box shut. (Note: Bring duct tape.) Then have a thirty-pack shot-put challenge for distance. Call it a test of manhood.

Speed Round
Players must sink their ball fastest. Watch out for flying balls in this round. Whoever sinks their ball first and fastest wins.

THE ZOOLANDER PARTY

Every decade has one dominating photo pose. The '50s had bunny ears. The '60s had the peace sign. The '70s had Travolta's *Saturday Night Fever* pose. The '80s had the Lionel Richie (relive the glory on page 204). The '90s brought us Triple H's "suck it." And the 2000s were dominated by Derek Zoolander's "Blue Steel." Every Facebook page in America has at least one of these really, really, ridiculously good pictures. It's time for you and your friends to crown the VH1 Male and Female Fashion Model of the Year.

THE SET-UP

Set up a well-lit backdrop for fashion photos. Appoint a fashion photographer for the night and make sure he gets "Blue Steel" shots of everyone. Make sure your house/venue has enough room for a runway. The pinnacle of the night is the walk-off. Nominate three judges for the party. They will award one male and one female winner based on the following categories: costume, photo pose, and walk off.

Models can't have their spines looking fat. Keep the drinks healthy. Some good options are white wine sangria, Zima, Michelob Ultra, Blackberry Sunsets (love those antioxidants), Zyr Vodka, Mango Bellinis, Pomegranate Cosmo Shots, and—of course—Orange Mocha Frappuccinos (orange sherbert, vanilla ice cream, and spiced rum).

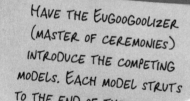

HAVE THE EUGOOGOOLIZER (MASTER OF CEREMONIES) INTRODUCE THE COMPETING MODELS. EACH MODEL STRUTS TO THE END OF THE CATWALK AND THEN HAS TEN SECONDS TO IMPRESS THE JUDGES. THIS CAN BE A PHOTO POSE, DANCE MOVE OR HIDDEN TALENT.

DRESS THE PART

Male or female, it doesn't matter. It's fashion. Try out tinted glasses, headbands, leather pants, fur coats, Native American face paint, capri pants, velour jump suits, fuzzy snow boots, multiple-popped collars, sexy coal miners, mermaid/merman, shoulder pad suits, and derelict clothing (fashion inspired by homeless vagrants).

PLAYLIST

Perfect for hitting the runway:

"Relax"
Frankie Goes to Hollywood

"I Love My Sex"
Benny Benassi

"I'm Bossy"
Kelis

"Venus "
Bananarama

"Simply Irresistible"
Robert Palmer

"That's Not My Name"
The Ting Tings

"Free Your Mind"
En Vogue

"Fergalicious"
Fergie

"Louis Vuitton Mix"
Daft Punk

"Dior Homme Mix"
Justice

Derek Zoolander became famous with his camera pose, Blue Steel. 5th Year has traveled from the West Virginia coalmines to the Hollywood red carpets to compile this list of twenty revolutionary camera poses.

1. **Forrest Gump Pose:** Eyes closed, mouth open, with a peace sign

2. **Drunkleberry Finn:** Hike your pants up as high as possible and do buck teeth

3. **Finger Moustache:** Draw on inside of index finger and place over top lip

4. **Awkward Prom Pose:** Guy behind girl with hands on her hips (surprised looks for both)

5. **Mexican Prom Pose:** Group shot with some mean mugging and b-boy stances

6. **Offensive Line Pose:** Make sure there is one quarterback under the center

7. **Human Pyramid:** The closest thing to a college orgy in the '50s

8. **Yoga Pose:** Downward dogs and flying lotuses

9. **I'm on Ecstasy Pose:** Messy hair, sensually touching own body, and eyes rolled up

10. **Air Guitar Pose:** Midair shredding pic

11. **Asian Tourist Pose:** Eyes closed, giggling, with two peace signs

12. Lionel Ritchie Pose*: Laying down on ground with elbow and leg propped up.

13. Fat Kid Face: Use both hands to squish your cheeks forward then lick your lips

14. I Just Walked in on My Parents Having Sex Pose: Unspeakable horror and disgust

15. I Just Won the Lottery Pose: Opposite of above—pure celebration

16. Fist in Mouth Pose: Who's got the biggest mouth?

17. Fake Smile Pose: You're hung over and Aunty Kathy is pestering you for a picture

18. *Weekend at Bernie's* Pose: Two people holding up a dead person with sunglasses on

19. Indie Rock Album Cover Pose: Random geographical arrangement of vague expressions

20. Sears Ad Pose: Super-cheesy 1990s kneeling down modeling stance

*THE LIONEL RICHIE POSE

Absolute genius. For those of you who don't know about this historically groundbreaking pose, prepare for enlightenment. No other man in the history of pop music will ever have chart topping singles, a jerry curl, and an economics degree from a prestigious school. Plain and simple, Lionel Richie is a man's man who can lie on his side in a striped sweater and still ooze heterosexuality.

To commemorate Lionel's existence, start making every person that enters your house take a photo in the Lionel Richie pose. We got the idea from sketch comedians *www.JoeyandDavid.com* and ran with it. Place the photos above your mantel.

WHEN A NEWCOMER ENTERS YOUR HOUSE IT'S A MANDATORY RITE OF PASSAGE TO GET A PHOTO TAKEN IN THE POSE. IT'S A GREAT ICEBREAKER FOR HOUSE PARTIES.

OPERATION GET YOUR LIFE BACK TOGETHER

You've just thrown a party. Your house looks like a combination of the city dump and a Vietnamese battlefield. Half-drank beers and crushed red cups are everywhere. There's definitely puke in and around the toilet. Some guy that you don't know is in his boxers sporting morning wood on the couch. You need your house back; it's '80s movie cleaning montage time.

After a house party leaves its skid marks all over your already shitty abode, its time to take action. It's not easy at first. Waking up is tough. Your eyes lids are crusted shut and you know when you open them, eyelashes will stingingly be ripped from your face. Movement brings body pain. Head, arms, neck, and legs . . . all sore as shit. *What the hell did you do to yourself?* On top of the various UDIs causing you pain, your house is a fucking mess. Time to get to work. Being lazy and sitting in your disgusting sty of a home will only make you depressed.

UDI: Unidentified drinking injury.

Your goal for the next two hours is to get your house back to ground zero. Here's how you start. Open your blinds, windows, and doors. Let some fresh air mix with the puke stank that has been festering in the house for the last six hours. Wake up the passed out degenerates by throwing garbage at them. Delegate tasks and crank the music. Music is an important factor in the cleaning process. People will feel shitty about all the stupid things they did and said the night before, so pad the hangover and embarrassment with good tunes.

10 Good Hungover-Cleaning Music Suggestions

1. Gogol Bordello
2. N.A.S.A.
3. Edward Sharpe and the Magnetic Zeroes
4. Major Lazer
5. Felt
6. Mosdub.com
7. Neon Indian
8. Gorillaz
9. Mylo
10. Mixes from *www.thehoodinternet.com*

Next, focus on the big stuff. Go after the big garbage first like cans, boxes, bottles, food, dishes, and dead animals. There will be a potpourri of crap laying everywhere. Don't get distracted by the immensity of the task, one cup of cigarette butt beer at a time. I like to be really annoying during the cleaning process; pretend you're still drunk, or crack a few light beers, and start making jokes and signing. All of sudden, the party is way more fun than it was last night. I recommend you use a "piss bucket." You'll run into countless amounts of unfinished beer and Coke colored beverages. Instead of going to the sink every time you have to pour something out, or throwing full beers into a leaking garbage bag, dump the drinks into a central bucket. (Your tapped keg's ice bucket makes a good piss bucket.) And the genius of it is that the bucket can move from room to room with you.

Piss Bucket: A homemade reservoir of unfinished drinks.

Consolidate the garbage in garbage bags and bring all the dishes to the kitchen sink. Pile that sink high and

WHEN YOU'RE THROWING SHIT AWAY, DON'T BE SHY—THIS IS A GOOD CHANCE TO GET RID OF NONPARTY CRAP THAT'S BEEN TAKING UP ROOM.

IF YOU'RE PARTY SPILLED OUTSIDE, MAKE SURE YOU CLEAN UP ANY BOTTLES, GLASSES, AND BUTTS LITTERING YOUR BACKYARD.

don't worry about them until later. Bring your garbage bags outside. Give the bags full of bottles and cans to a homeless person. Remember, one man's trash is another man's Steel Reserve tallboy.

Hopefully, your house is now sans garbage and clutter and you can start getting into the shitty gritty of it. Chances are, your house is covered in a sticky layer of alcohol and sugar. The smell is literally stuck to the floors. Sweep the floors first. Then it's time for my best friend, ammonia. No bacteria can survive the wrath of Dictator Ammonia. I prefer the lemon-scented variety; it will give your house a nice motherly touch in the midst of an apocalyptic melee of destruction. Put the ammonia in some spray bottles and douse your house. It works great on the countertops and floors. Use an old towel as a mopping rag. Spray your floors with the ammonia, step on the towel, and pretend you're on a NordicTrack. Your body weight erases spots better than any mop could *and* you get some exercise. It's a win-win.

Now you're getting somewhere. The house appears to be getting clean. Light a few candles to get the place smelling decent. By now, all your guests should either be gone or pitching in. No one should be sleeping. It's time to get your living room back in working order. Couches and pillows should return to their respective places. Blankets should be folded and put in closets. Vacuum the shit out of your rugs and carpets if you have them; it's the only way to beat the Dorito crumbs. Have one of the stragglers start on the dishes. Do one last sweep of the bathrooms and bedrooms—take a deep breath and attack the nastiness. (It's always amazing, and disgusting, the type of crap that shows up in these spots.)

This has been a stressful morning. Your hands are wrinkled from sugar water and alcohol. Time for breakfast. Head to the nearest diner and stuff your face. Be sure to have a beer with breakfast—you just earned it.

THE 5TH YEAR CALENDAR

It's important to have something to look forward to—whether you're in school, at work, or sitting at home unemployed on Mom's couch. That's why we've put together the 5th Year Calendar. Now, no matter the time of year, you have a party to plan in the not-too-distant future. We've included the seasonal staples and it's your job to fill in this social calendar with the other ideas in the book. While it's important to celebrate the liberation of Ireland on March 17th with some green libations at your own English Oppression Day festivity, it's equally important to celebrate your own holiday every year with good friends, good times, and a great party.

ANAL PARTY, I MEAN, *ANNUAL* PARTY

Throwing an annual party (and not on your birthday, you selfish asshole) that you can call your own keeps the dream alive. What dream? The dream of delivering a day of reckless entertainment to your friends—forever. Be the one to start a tradition that lives on for a million years.

There are 365 days in a year. Most of these days are spent doing the unimportant things—class, work, laundry, exercising, drinking water. All crap. None of the other days compare to the one special day a year you look forward to—your annual party. You've spent 364 days getting ready for it. It is the one day you absolutely know, without a doubt, you are going to partake in some kind of amazing debauchery.

Stick with one theme that remains the same every year, but add new traditions and modifications. Like old jockey underwear, an annual party gets better with age. Adding new traditions to your annual party will make every year you throw it more amazing than the last.

When you throw your annual party there are basic party planning details to cover. First, give it a name. You have to call it something if you plan to do this every year, so make sure the name isn't generic bullshit. It should be funny and descriptive and incorporate the theme. The name should get people excited to show up. And again, you need to make the theme specific to each individual year. The general theme will get the people to the door, but getting your friends to shit their pants in joy every year means you party has to offer something new. Supplement the general theme with new activities. For example, at your annual All-American Day, this year's specific event could be a Race to America Regatta. Competitors race in homemade boats to a watering hole on a lake, where they will spend the afternoon drinking sailor hooch and denouncing the queen in true patriotic fashion.

Get your circle of degenerates involved in throwing annual parties so that there's something special to look forward to all year. February is the Fake Wake. May is Prom in Your Prime. July is Beach Bunker Bonanza. September is the United Nations Party. And so forth and so on. If you throw a good enough annual party, it'll be looked forward to like Christmas by kids—like a beer-soaked, raging Christmas. It'll be a tradition so unique that it would take some serious gonasyphaluherpecrabs to keep people from attending.

If we don't have something to look forward to in life, we'll die—which is why parties exist, to keep us alive.

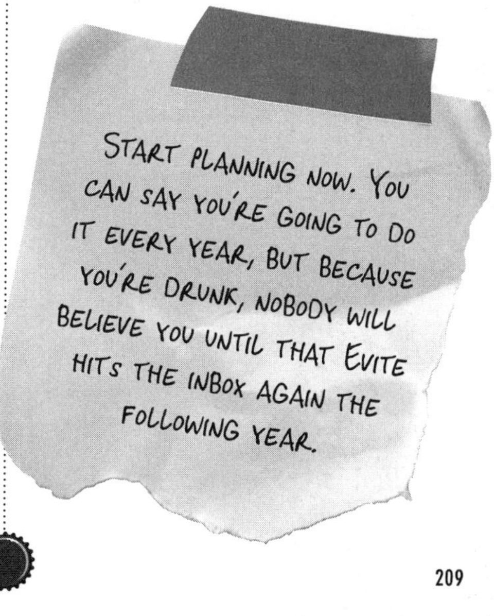
START PLANNING NOW. YOU CAN SAY YOU'RE GOING TO DO IT EVERY YEAR, BUT BECAUSE YOU'RE DRUNK, NOBODY WILL BELIEVE YOU UNTIL THAT EVITE HITS THE INBOX AGAIN THE FOLLOWING YEAR.

January

DAY	PARTY
1	New Year Detox: Typically after New Year's Eve—and the holiday bender
2	leading up to it—it's nice to take a breather from aggressive partying. Spend at
3	least a week exercising and not consuming; start your year off mildly healthy.
4	
5	
6	
7	
8	
9	
10	
11	
12	
13	
14	
15	
16	
17	
18	
19	
20	
21	
22	
23	
24	Royal Rumble Party: You've had a few weeks since New Year's Eve, so you should be
25	feeling better by now. Time to thaw the corn dogs and stock up on cheap beer, 'cause
26	it's wrastlin' time! The WWE's Royal Rumble usually happens the last weekend of the
27	month, so plan around that.
28	
29	
30	
31	

> Obviously these dates won't match up with weekends every year. That's okay. These are just general dates for when certain shenanigans should go down. Plan yours on the day that works best for you and your friends.

February

DAY	PARTY
1	
2	
3	
4	Euro Trash Bash: Hans! Yuri! Sven! Come over and show
5	me your strudels!
6	
7	
8	
9	
10	
11	
12	
13	
14	
15	
16	
17	
18	
19	
20	
21	
22	
23	Flip Camera Film Fest: Organize this event the same weekend the Academy Awards
24	are being held. This way, you and your friends can make arrogant comments about the
25	difficulties of filmmaking while they're handing out the Oscars.
26	
27	
28	
29	

Don't forget to write in the annual parties you and your friends plan on making yearly traditions.

March	
DAY	PARTY
1	
2	
3	
4	
5	
6	
7	
8	
9	
10	
11	
12	
13	
14	
15	
16	
17	English Oppression Day: It is on this day that the Red Coats really like to let those
18	drunken Irishmen know who their Imperial daddies really are . . . and the day that
19	those drunken Irishmen like to get really drunk.
20	
21	
22	
23	
24	Leprechaun Extravaganza: What better way to end all the St. Patrick's Day festivities
25	than by chasing a little ginger leprechaun through campus?
26	
27	
28	
29	
30	bEaster Egg Hunt: Those crazy Christians are always changing the date that Easter
31	occurs. It's typically late March or early April. Hold your Hunt the weekend after.

April

DAY	PARTY
1	
2	
3	
4	
5	
6	Wedding Crashers: Break the mold of penis veils and cosmopolitans and do something
7	different. April is a romanctical month for this party, whether or not one of your
8	friends is headed down the aisle.
9	
10	
11	
12	
13	
14	
15	
16	Ro-Sham-Bo Tournament: Great to throw directly after NCAA Madness since your
17	friends are still craving that victory bracket.
18	
19	
20	
21	
22	
23	
24	
25	
26	
27	
28	
29	Day at the Track: The grass is green, the horses are fed—time to dust off those hats
30	and get to the track. Any warm April afternoon works perfectly for this event.

May

DAY	PARTY
1	
2	
3	
4	
5	Toma Todo! A Cinco de Drinko Dinner Party:
6	Forget going to the bar to celebrate Mexican
7	independence—way too crowded. Organize a
8	tequila-filled night-in with your friends instead.
9	
10	
11	
12	
13	
14	
15	
16	
17	
18	
19	
20	
21	
22	
23	
24	
25	
26	All-American Day: Memorial Day is a day for celebrating America and how much we love
27	to eat frozen foods, sport Wranglers, and hoot 'n holler.
28	
29	
30	
31	

Don't get us wrong, bars are fun. But it's better to avoid them during amateur-hour holidays like Cinco de Mayo.

June

DAY	PARTY
1	
2	
3	
4	OUTDOOR CONCERT: TIME TO GET OUTSIDE FOR SOME WARM WEATHER DANCING AND DRINKING.
5	ANY WEEKEND IN JUNE IS A GREAT TIME TO THROW THIS EVENT.
6	
7	
8	
9	
10	
11	
12	
13	NEON OR NOTHING: HEAD TO THE RIVER AND GET YOUR CANOES WET . . . IF YOU KNOW WHAT
14	I MEAN.
15	
16	
17	
18	
19	
20	
21	
22	MCCONAUGHAVEN!: WOODERSON SAYS TO GET
23	OFF YOUR ASS AND THROW THIS PARTY—IN HIS
24	HONOR. YOU SHOULD TRY TO TIME IT WITH YOUR
25	AREA'S LAST DAY OF SCHOOL.
26	
27	
28	
29	
30	

July

DAY	PARTY
1	
2	
3	
4	Citizenship Party: What better way to celebrate America than throw a party in honor
5	of those people who built this country.
6	
7	
8	
9	
10	
11	
12	
13	
14	
15	Zoolander Party: Chisel those pecs, emasculate yourself everyway you can, and buy
16	some sensitive undies . . . the summer's the perfect time to throw this party for really,
17	really, ridiculously good-looking people.
18	
19	
20	
21	Romance Novel Party: You'll need some warm weather for this one 'cause your shirt is
22	definitely not staying on.
23	
24	
25	
26	
27	
28	
29	
30	
31	

August

DAY	PARTY
1	
2	
3	
4	
5	WILLIAM WALLACE INVITATIONAL: SCOTTS DO GOLF, AND SCOTTS DO KILLING . . . SO UNSHEATHE
6	YOUR CLUBS AND CHARGE A FAIRWAY ANY WEEKEND IN AUGUST.
7	
8	
9	
10	
11	
12	
13	
14	
15	
16	
17	
18	
19	
20	BEER OLYMPICS: SUMMER'S COME TO AN END. YOU'VE PARTIED A LOT THESE LAST FEW MONTHS, BUT
21	WHO'S PARTIED THE HARDEST? SOUNDS LIKE YOU'LL NEED TO HOLD THE OLYMPICS TO FIGURE OUT
22	THE VICTOR.
23	
24	
25	
26	
27	
28	
29	
30	
31	

September

DAY	PARTY
1	
2	
3	
4	
5	
6	
7	
8	
9	
10	
11	
12	
13	
14	Prom in Your Prime: It's back to school—if you're still actually in school. If not, it's a
15	good time to pretend you're a pimply faced freshman.
16	
17	
18	
19	
20	
21	
22	
23	
24	
25	Brown Bag Surprise Party: Bags, bags,
26	bags, and more bags of who the hell
27	knows what. Bring some excitement to a
28	boring fall weekend with this shitshow.
29	
30	

October

DAY	PARTY
1	
2	
3	
4	
5	
6	
7	
8	
9	
10	
11	
12	
13	
14	Tour de Franzia: It's harvest time. The vineyards have been picked, the crush is on, and
15	the wine you'll be drinking at this event will make you crap your pants until Halloween.
16	
17	
18	
19	
20	
21	
22	
23	
24	
25	
26	
27	
28	
29	
30	Last-Minute Halloween: Don't plan some skanky night at the local club. Substitute a
31	night of lines and obnoxious drunk kids for a last-minute success.

November

DAY	PARTY
1	
2	
3	
4	
5	
6	
7	
8	
9	
10	
11	Vietnam Vet Party: Celebrate the men and women who served our country this
12	Veteran's Day by throwing a party in their honor.
13	
14	
15	
16	
17	
18	
19	
20	
21	Donkey Punch Dinner Party: Keep stuffing
22	the turkey between you and your family.
23	In order to celebrate Thanksgiving with
24	your friends, organize a different kind of
25	dinner party.
26	
27	
28	
29	
30	

It's a good idea to set up your own version of holiday celebrations with your friends. It should help curb the drinking at your family functions.

December

DAY	PARTY
1	
2	
3	
4	
5	
6	
7	
8	Meat Baby: This holiday is for a different
9	kind of god—the kind that delivers you bags
10	of meat at night. Do not disappoint.
11	
12	
13	
14	
15	
16	
17	
18	
19	
20	
21	Hallow-Thank-Mas Eve: There are just too many holidays to celebrate with everyone,
22	so in December, make sure to throw this all-encompassing holiday event.
23	
24	
25	
26	
27	
28	
29	
30	
31	

Perfect for any day during the holiday season, except Christmas.

ART CREDITS

Bottle cap © istockphoto / FreeTransform

Dice © istockphoto / lushik

Notepaper © istockphoto / Pannonia

MP3 player © istockphoto / anzlyldrm

Balloons © istockphoto / bubaone

Hanger © Neubau Welt

Large group of people, © istockphoto / TrapdoorMedia, page x

Crowd waving, © istockphoto / GrafiStart, page xiii

Picnic table, © Neubau Welt, page 3

Happy Aussie, © istockphoto / Kolbz, page 7

Crocodile, © istockphoto / Ace_Create, page 9

People doing funny faces, © istockphoto / knape, page 10

Cross hair, © istockphoto / sasimoto, page 15

Easter Bunny, © istockphoto / EventureMan, page 17

Ping pong table, © NeuBau Welt, page 21

Garbage dumpster, © istockphoto / Casarsa, page 23

Guns, © istockphoto / packagedesign, page 24

Hippie smokers, © istockphoto / JennaWagner, page 25

Basketball, © istockphoto / sasimoto, page 26

Cell phone, © istockphoto / pa3x, page 27

Remote control, © istockphoto / boroda003, page 27

Disco dancer, © istockphoto / GAZ1DAN, page 29

Clown, © istockphoto / G-o-o-d-M-a-n, page 30

Pirate, © istockphoto / selimaksan, page 32

Pirate silhouette, © istockphoto / hypergon, page 33

Friends toasting, © istockphoto / nuno, page 35

Drunk man, © istockphoto / Smithore, page 39

Man with burger, © istockphoto / THEPALMER, page 43

Traditional hat toss, © istockphoto / ericsphotography, page 49

Fashionable Woman, © istockphoto / Illustrious, page 54

Binoculars, © Neubau Welt, page 55

Croquet, © istockphoto / step2626, page 56

Bottle, © Neubau Welt, pages ii and 62

Muscle boy, © istockphoto / Stalman, page 64

Guy, © Neubau Welt, page 65

Kids, © Neubau Welt, page 67

Couple, © istockphoto / bjones27, page 69

Duct tape, © istockphoto / Devonyu, page 72

St. Patrick's Day, © istockphoto / nuno, page 74

Dead narco, © istockphoto / JordiDelgado, page 81

Friends, © istockphoto / Spanic, page 83

Businessman, © istockphoto / anouchka, page 85

Drunk reindeer, © istockphoto / PeskyMonkey, page 87

Street light, © Neubau Welt, page 90

Denim jacket, © istockphoto / dmodly, page 92

White trash, © istockphoto / Renphoto, page 96

Leprechaun, © istockphoto / RyanJLane, page 99

Diving, © istockphoto / ActionPics, page 101

Party, © istockphoto / Gizmo, page 103

Steak, © istockphoto / bjones27, page 105

Bodybuilder, © istockphoto / vuk8691, page 107

Minigolf, © istockphoto / davidbuehn, page 119

Golfers, © istockphoto / AndersonAnderson, pages 120 and 121

Nerd, © istockphoto / RyanJLane, page 122

Singing women, © istockphoto / elkor, page 125

Tripod, © Neubau Welt, page 128

Folding chair, © Neubau Welt, page 130

Video gamers, © istockphoto / jacomstephens, page 134

Barbecue, © istockphoto / chemc, page 136

Summer party, © istockphoto / Ladida, page 138

Knife and fork, © Neubau Welt, page 143

Red wine, © istockphoto / kzenon, page 154

Boxing ring, © istockphoto / freie-kreation, page 159

Wooden puzzle, © istockphoto / muratsen, page 162

Party picture, © istockphoto / MichaelDeLeon, page 164

Lineup, © istockphoto / VikaValter, page 172

Tequila shot, © istockphoto / A_N, page 181

Bicycle, © Neubau Welt, page 185

Double decker bus, © istockphoto / Bim, page 186

Flags, © istockphoto / yesfoto, page 188

Young man, © istockphoto / PeterPolak, page 191

Girlfriends, © istockphoto / CraigSwatton, page 194

Roller rink, © istockphoto / cjmckendry, page 196

Golfer, © istockphoto / Fitzer, page 199

Models, © istockphoto / Claudiad, page 201

ABOUT THE AUTHORS

Connor Pritchard partied with the Jesuits at Loyola Marymount University and now makes a living writing in LA. He and his coauthor Dominic are two of the men behind Comedy Central's *Workaholics*. And if Shrek and Van Wilder had a love child, it would be Connor.

Dominic Russo is a comedy writer and producer who studied the art of partying during five years at Arizona State University. With his coauthor and cohort Connor, he founded The 5th Year brand, which strives to make life fun for everyone. He continues to live like a college student in Los Angeles.